Not Too Young For Wonder

California Poets in the Schools 2023 State Anthology

Brennan DeFrisco, Editor
Fernando Albert Salinas, Assistant Editor
Meg Hamill, Executive Director

The title of this anthology, *Not Too Young For Wonder*,
is adapted from a poem by Amy Liu

Cover Art by Mayra Tello Hernandez

California Poets in the Schools
P.O. Box 1328
Santa Rosa, CA 95402
   Meg Hamill, Executive Director
   David Sibbet, President of the Board

ISBN: 978-0-939927-31-9

Each time I write a poem, I recommit in some way to the world.

Ada Limón

CONTENTS

To engage in poetry is to uncover the most vulnerable aspects of our lives and confront the challenges of our worlds. It was not until I engaged in poetry myself–both studying the art form and creating my own work–that I discovered the true power of a pen. Poetry became my outlet for self-expression and a gateway to discovering my passion for mentoring youth and uplifting the voices of my community through writing. As a former mentee, being a Poet-Teacher is one of the greatest joys I've experienced thus far in my career. I have watched the quietest students grow the volume of their voice, the most stubborn students discover a love for writing, and the shyest students find a home in the performing arts over the years. Poetry, above all, is a unifying force that brings students of all ages and identities together.

The students published within this anthology range from elementary school to high school age, and the youthfulness within these pages is simultaneously filled with hope and sorrow, assertiveness and modesty. Above all, these poets are boldly honest about their self-images, self-expressions, and perceptions of the world around them. They do as a true writer must: unapologetically let their voices guide their pen to the page. Indeed, a writer may be nurtured at any age, and this collection does well in demonstrating the timelessness of one's connection with art. In the midst of a troubled world, these writers prove their wisdom and power within their poetry, offering themselves–both literally and metaphorically–to the reader.

To not only write from the heart, but to submit a piece to be published is no small task, especially for those who find more confidence through written word (as opposed to spoken). It is our duty, then, to grant these young voices an audience, to soak in their words, and to celebrate the journeys that led them to these pages. As one student writes, "we are not too young for wonder, / And knowing, knowing our word's weight: / We must, and we will, create."

As mentors, it is our hope to guide our students to hold their pens as fearlessly as their heads and teach them how to face adversity in stride. It is clear from these poems that the youth of this generation will carry the world forward with fierce minds and strong hearts. It is my honor to commend these students in claiming their place in the poetic world, as well as the Poet-Teachers who support their creative journeys.

Angelina Leaños
Ventura County Youth Poet Laureate Emeritus

When My Name Is Spoken

I Am A Story

I am from a tall city with thick fog
moist skies but dry land
the fires that rage
and the sprouts that follow

I am the fireflies caught in a jar
and the grasshoppers
disrupting the quiet night

bright red strawberries
sprinkled with freckles
gathered in a basket
so small, but so sweet

I am a breath of cool air
on a December night
the stars hung above and
wispy clouds passing by

the steady murmurs of blue and green waters
pink skin and sandy feet
silver shells and
smooth green glass
abandoned on the beach

I am the protest posters
colorful and loud
stubborn and headstrong

held up by those around me
each monumental to my cause

I am a story
that's still being written
an unfinished puzzle
pieces scattered on the table,
the bigger picture still incomplete

Milena Garrone, Grade 9
Lowell High School, San Francisco County
Angelina Cowan-Byrns, Classroom Teacher
Susan Terence, Poet-Teacher

I Am

I'm as happy as a baby labradoodle playing in daisies
but as sad as rain pouring down hard.

I'm as tough as a tiger prowling down in grass
but as delicate as a rose petal blowing in the wind.

I'm as fast as a cheetah searching the savannah
but as slow as a snail slowly slithering.

I'm as curious as a kitten pawing at its mom
but I know as much as an elephant.

I'm as strong as a lion
but as weak as a mouse.

I'm a puzzle and the words are the pieces,
put them together and me's what will be.

Charlotte Duckhorn, Grade 3
Apple Blossom Elementary School, Sonoma County
Amy McLoone, Classroom Teacher
Lisa Shulman, Poet-Teacher

This is Me

I am from Frankie
and Carson, the family
games we play, the
four-hour road trips
we make, and the risks we take.

I am from dribbling the orange
rubber basketball across the
court, tippie-toeing across
the beam, and handstands
on the mat.

I am from the ginger in
gingerbread men and the yellowness
on the mac and cheese.

I am from the dreamland
in my head when I drift off
to sleep and dream
of beautiful things.

I am from the tall mountains with
the sage green color beaming on top,
the oak tree I hang on,
the daisies blooming in my backyard.

This is me.

Sadie Cole, Grade 5
Pleasant Valley Elementary School, Marin County
Angela Villaluna, Classroom Teacher
Lea Aschkenas, Poet-Teacher

My Heart

My heart is me and this is me
Inside my heart is a snowy mountain
that is so tall and hard to climb,
it will take forever to climb it
My heat carries warm, cuddly, love
My heart is made out of my loving friends and family
My heart is hungry for galaxies and stars
My heart sounds like powerful wolves howling
My heart feels like the fuzziest wolf fur ever

Ashlyn Loftus, Grade 4
Prestwood Elementary School, Sonoma County
Nichole Roberts, Classroom Teacher
Sandra Anfang, Poet-Teacher

I Am

I am a snake slithering through the desert
I am a tree growing
I am the wind pushing the clouds
I am the kid that has no color
I am an owl flying silently through the trees
I am a flower all pretty and beautiful
I am the sun shining down on all the lands

Caleb Birch, Grade 3
Mountain View Elementary School, Santa Barbara County
Holly Bosse, Classroom Teacher
Cie Gumucio, Poet-Teacher

Just Because

Just because I'm tall
    Doesn't mean I play basketball
    Or that I always have to be in the back
    It also means I can't always see over everyone
    Why do I need to be shorter?
    Should it matter to you?

Just because I'm tall
    Doesn't mean I'll be tall forever
    And that I don't fit in crowds
    I am not a daddy long leg spider
    Or even more mature than the other kids

Just because I'm tall
    Still means I'm the same age as other kids my age
    And I am not bigfoot
    Being tall isn't a bad thing,
    But people make it seem like it is.
    I don't think I need to be told I'm tall 24/7,
    It's annoying.

Just because I'm tall, please don't stereotype me.

Addison Lord, Grade 6
Willowside Middle School, Sonoma County
Nicola Niedermair, Classroom Teacher
Brennan DeFrisco, Poet-Teacher

My Voice

I am not afraid to use
my voice. You have never
heard it so let me tell you
it is soft, but non-stopping.
It is not used to the
quietness. It sounds like the trees
rustling in the wind.
My voice is like the
creek rippling. It is like
the gentle rain falling
from the sky.

My voice is the song of a bird.

Iris Jones, Grade 5
Murphy Elementary School, Humboldt County
Jamie Ellsmore, Classroom Teacher
Dan Zev Levinson, Poet-Teacher

The Name That Flies Over The River

My name sounds like the river's riffles
My name feels like feathers from the kingfisher bird
My name comes from the Yurok language
My name means kingfisher bird from the Klamath River
When my name is spoken, the fish fear, the river runs,
The deer dance, my name is Chey-lel'

Chey-lel' O'Neill, Grade 6
Blue Lake Elementary School, Humboldt County
Jenn Soderfelt, Classroom Teacher
Dan Zev Levinson, Poet-Teacher

I Am Finn

Hello
I am Finn
I am fun
I like to run
I am in a park with trees
that stand taller than me
I am with strangers who I don't know
I am on grass that blows in the wind
I am a human with a beloved family
I am a friend
I am with the wind that blows my hair and clothes
I am with benches that I (and others) can sit on
I am with birds that sing their song
I am with paper and a pen
I am living

Finn Hernandez, Grade 3
OEA Strike Solidarity School, Alameda County
Brennan DeFrisco, Poet-Teacher

I Am Alive

I sat there at my desk on January 12, 2023.
The time is 9:44pm now.
Somehow, I feel empty after completing my poems
for a school project, but why?
Because my heart only leaked on one poem.
That poem was extra credit.

I am a poet in some ways, and yet I gasp
for each word I catch in my throat, locked away.
Each word comes together as I write.
My voice is silenced by people I care for.
What is the point of caring?
or making the best of life?
Caring only breaks me more every day.
Life is short and makin' the most of it
will not help you through it
Life is painful, like drowning in the ocean of words
that only makes you sad 'til you are stuck in that feeling,
until you are once depressed for eternity.
But we humans live through it all without help.
Why can't life be simple once again?
when we didn't know that pain existed.
But as I said, it's too late for that.
We put this on ourselves.

The world will eat you up if you let it.
Why is the world so cruel?
The world doesn't want us to live happily

And yet, I am here:
Alive, awake, breathing slowly,
hearing my heart pump blood in a rhythm.
I am here.
Not with you.
But here, on this planet called Earth.
In the Milky Way, spinning around forever.
Alive.

I am alive.

Eleanor Giada B. Ceccarelli, Grade 6
Willowside Middle School, Sonoma County
Cari Cardle, Classroom Teacher
Brennan DeFrisco, Poet-Teacher

An Ocean of Tears

Paint me as a girl crying on the stairs at night.
Paint me as my tears overwhelm me with loss.
Paint me as blue as the sea.
Paint me as the tiniest fish in the biggest ocean.
Paint my blonde hair with highlights of brown
Hanging over my face with shame.
Paint my eyes filled with tears.
Paint my freckles as brown as dirt.
Take my mouth dry as a desert.
Paint the ocean of my tears.
Paint me.

Sidney Sheehy, Grade 5
Alexander Valley School, Sonoma County
Christopher Bowen, Classroom Teacher
Maureen Hurley, Poet-Teacher

If You Knew

would you still love me if you knew that
i sneeze and snot pours from my nose
like whole rivers, unfortunate allergies
to the one thing always around: dust

would you still love me if you knew that
i wake with pimples, the plague of my face
that my hair tends to be tangled, and my
vision vanishes with each passing minute

would you still love me if you knew that
i am imperfect; that maybe i'm a little
broken inside, but aren't you too?

if you knew, would you still kiss me
like my soul is pure gold, my laughter
like sunshine bubbling over the pages
of my book as i look at you

if you knew every flaw that makes me, me
because no one can ever be perfect
would the moments still mean as much
as they now do to you?

if you knew, would you still hold me
like i am the second half of your heart
would you still pour out your dreams like
it's always been me you've seen in them

would you still love me if you knew that
i cry ugly, sobbing tears, staining my cheeks
with streaks of dark mascara - it's not pretty

but i am not just a pretty face, not just
a warm embrace; i am a heart, and a soul
who deserves to be loved as a whole
not just the shell you see on the outside

so, if you knew, would you still love me
the way that you do — would you?

Tashi Manchip, Grade 11
Tamalpais High School, Marin County
Barbara Ditz, Classroom Teacher
Maxine Flasher-Düzgüneş, Poet-Teacher

Glass

I am from broken glass,
from order and addiction,
the glue that held my parents together.
Living one life at home,
another at school.
Using my Spanish
but losing it too.
Pretending in front of
either friends or family.
A reflection of him
but never of her.
Never letting anyone in
Once in,
more glass breaks,
glass that can only be turned to sand
or shards that stab away at me
that I'll have to learn to live with.

Alexa Nuñez, Grade 12
Willits High School, Mendocino County
Katrina Hall, Classroom Teacher
Jabez W. Churchill, Poet-Teacher

The Door to My Heart

The door to my heart is made of shining black obsidian
which is locked with a golden padlock only I can open.
As you step into my heart, your eyes fall on a beautiful tree,
speckled with gold. Surrounding it is a beautiful moat
full of blue water, shimmering and reflecting the golden willow.
This room signifies sadness.

As you walk out, water splashing beneath your feet, you exit the
door. Soft music fills your ears and you follow it. As you walk into
the next room, you see a tall tree and another and another. You
realize it's a jungle. But this is no ordinary jungle: this is a poison
jungle. This room is fear.

Leaves crunch beneath your feet as you make your way to the next
door. Opening the door, you fall through onto soft, warm sand.
Standing up, your eyes fall on a wonderful, silver lake, outlined in
sand and mountains in every direction. You wade into the crisp,
cool lake, dive under, find the next door and open it, falling
through. This room is peace.

As your eyes adjust to the light, you see a beautiful flower field.
Millions of flowers in different colors, spread out over miles and
miles. This room is happiness.

You walk over to the next, flowers leaning out of your way.
You open the door and walk through. You see a volcano, dripping
with lava. Your feet are getting hotter by the second. You run,
looking for the door. The door has disappeared. You start to
panic, getting more and more frustrated the more you look.

Finally, you see an open door and walk over to it. You slowly inspect it and look through the doorway.

You see another field, but not the wildflower field. It is different, smaller, with grass. You walk through and flowers grow wherever you step. You get very surprised. Surrounded by flowers, you lay down and close your eyes. This room is surprise.

You think of all you have seen and open your eyes. You realize you're in your own room and you close your eyes, falling asleep into a peaceful dream of the crisp, cool lake and the flower field and the willow tree with the moat.

You are at peace as you slowly drift off.

Della McFarland, Grade 4
Hope Elementary School, Santa Barbara County
Michael Anderson, Classroom Teacher
Cie Gumucio, Poet-Teacher

Just Because I'm Quiet

Just because I'm quiet

> Doesn't mean I can't stand up,
> Or that I'm depressed.
> Doesn't mean I'm sensitive,
> Or that I'm not happy.

Just because I'm quiet

> Doesn't mean you should judge me.
> You can't make me tell you things that aren't true.
> Doesn't mean I have no friends.
> Do you think I'm a terrorist for being quiet?

Just because I'm quiet

> Doesn't mean I'm not paying attention,
> Doesn't mean I can't hear you.
> It doesn't mean I don't have feelings,
> Or that I can't speak.
> Doesn't mean I can't make a difference.

Just because I'm quiet, don't stereotype me.

Jessica Anaya Gayosso, Grade 6
Willowside Middle School, Sonoma County
Nicola Niedermair, Classroom Teacher
Brennan DeFrisco, Poet-Teacher

I Am

I am a great, big, monstrous beast inside,
your cold black heart, feeding on despair.

I am frost slowly soaking all the hope
and happiness, like a massive sponge.

I am a leaf floating away from the great oak tree.
I am a vast blue ocean hiding the beauty inside me—
I am a story that can never end.

Lucia Mitrousis, Grade 3
Vallecito School, Marin County
Dara Ferra, Classroom Teacher
Terri Glass, Poet-Teacher

My Heart

My heart is bigger than me
    so all I want to do is love.

My heart carries all my happiest moments
    and all my saddest moments.

My heart is made out of my funniest moments,
    all my happiest moments, my saddest moments,
    and all my angry moments.

My heart sounds like an elephant stomping in the wild.

My heart is me and that is the best part of it!

Makenna Balch-Miovas, Grade 4
Prestwood Elementary School, Sonoma County
Katie Grimes, Classroom Teacher
Sandra Anfang, Poet-Teacher

My Constant Heart

My heart pumps all of the liquid I bleed out
Containing myself, trying to pull through
the thing that keeps me alive
Writing and writing my emotions I feel
Shooting my heart with fireworks
Calling my heart to stop the pain
and the bleeding veins and the pain monitors
Crying I can do, but not always
A scar is forever, but a cut is for a bit
Still in pain, even with a cotton ball
To collect the redness squirting out of me
My constant heart won't stop
My heart needs love, but also scratches
Will it stop? No, because it is made out of me
Still, emotions I love:
Joy, anger, happiness, and action
are or can come on a daily basis
Shattered after fake love or broken into pieces
Time flies and I'm still alive
But even more grateful for the thing
that keeps me in this world, seeing colors and nature
Always full of surprises, ups and downs
My heart controls me with curiosity
Living I will always do in each other
Paying it forward with kindness and love
But on one special day, when
Everyone experiences love in a certain way

Somehow my soul will never stop from going to new places
and new adventures to stop by on my way through life
My heart controls and is made out of me
I am made out of love and my emotions
and most of all, my lively, colorful spirit

Nora Bottari, Grade 4
Prestwood Elementary School, Sonoma County
Nichole Roberts, Classroom Teacher
Sandra Anfang, Poet-Teacher

Magnolias, Butterflies, Poppies, and Roses

I come from humid days, farmland, and cold nights.
My brothers and sisters sprouted like greens, carrots,
and blossomed like sweet southern magnolias.
The taste of teacakes, black-eyed peas, and collard greens.
My feet are anchored like the roots of a tree on the banks of
the Mississippi River.
The land I inherited from my parents, Magee and George
Tomson, my providers who reward me with the fruits
of their labor.
My siblings and I grew like peas in a pod.
I see the fear of my family as my uncles were sent to war.
And the relief is like a cool summer breeze when they return.
I feel no fear when we move and migrate like monarch
butterflies sprouting their wings and taking flight,
Setting off to an unknown future to pursue new opportunities
The transformation from sweet magnolias to golden poppy,
But sadness when leaving some of my flight behind.

My children grew up like golden California poppies
With their Diamond golden pedals
I am a Great Tree. I have come to provide nourishment,
guidance, sustenance, and shade for my children
and their children's children.
I am a great rose bush that many have sprouted from,
with all the beautiful colors, a rose bush
that spans across Generations.

I am my family
and my family faith
and my family is me.

Renae Williams, Grade 9
Lowell High School, San Francisco County
Anne Torres, Classroom Teacher
Susan Terence, Poet-Teacher

Just Because I'm Latina

Just because I'm Latina,
> Doesn't mean I'm an English learner
> I'm as good as you at English
> I prefer to speak Spanish
> The importance of it matters
> Have you tried speaking Spanish?
> It's difficult, isn't it?

Just because I'm Latina,
> Doesn't mean I'm a migrant worker
> Don't think I'm a bad person
> Shouldn't mean I'm poor
> Don't expect me to listen to others, have my head low
> Do not assume I don't belong here.

Just because I'm Latina,
> Doesn't mean I have no rights
> I don't eat tacos every day, if you assume
> Don't assume I have weird foods and traditions
> I'm Latina and I'm proud of it.

Just because I'm Latina, don't judge me.

Victoria Hernandez, Grade 6
Willowside Middle School, Sonoma County,
Nicola Niedermair, Classroom Teacher
Brennan DeFrisco, Poet-Teacher

I'm From

I'm from bikes and running to the paletero,
from weekend trips to Mexico,
from moving place to place.

I'm from my mom's big garden,
from birthday parties where my mom cooked
and my brothers got drunk.

I am from:
Te van a jalar los pies,
if you don't listen to your mom.

I am from Ukiah and Puebla.

Hector Jimenez, Grade 11
South Valley High School, Mendocino County
Kita Grinberg, Classroom Teacher
Jabez W. Churchill, Poet-Teacher

Haiku

I am from young love
summer fairs
and stupid teen parents.

Bella Cruz, Grade 10
South Valley High School, Mendocino County
Kita Grinberg, Classroom Teacher
Jabez W. Churchill, Poet-Teacher

We

We are a group
that can collaborate
in many different ways

We want to be Pokémon,
a Gengar or the strongest one

We are constellations
because we are connected
in some ways

We are Patrick Mahomes,
we have cool hair,
good control,
and throw footballs like a Pokéball

We are poets –
kind-of good ones,
but we need to practice to get better

Group Poem, Grades 3-5
OEA Strike Solidarity School, Alameda County
Brennan DeFrisco, Poet-Teacher

I Am Perfect

I am perfect
I am a football player
I am a brick and never break
I am a bear and perfect as a dog
I am used for sports,
I am brave as a lion and smarter than a snake
I want to be a NFL player.
I used to be a lion but now I'm a gorilla
I am a gorilla you are a lion
I am a dog and help people cross the street
I am flying colors in school

Hayden Jenkins, Grade 3
Chenoweth Elementary School, Merced County
Meuy Saeteurn, Classroom Teacher
Dawn Trook, Poet-Teacher

Morning Moods

When I wake up in the morning
I'm as droopy as a wilted rose
My eyes are as drowsy as a koala.
I feel as tired as a sleepy sloth

but my legs feel light like air.

Victor Aguirre, Grade 4
Logan Memorial Educational Campus, San Diego County
Nate Herron, Classroom Teacher
Johnnierenee Nia Nelson, Poet-Teacher

Move

I'm bored.
I'm sleepy.
But, I'm at school learning.

I'm dreaming of building forts
inside a screen,
relaxing and listening to Ricco,
writing a letter to my mom.

Give my thoughts a rest.
Close my eyes.
I dream of having a good family,
then wake up—
take a run around the hood.
I make my way back home,
letting the water drench me,
then make my way back to school.

My hope is to move my momma
out of the hood!

Benny Hernandez, Grade 7
Isbell Middle School, Ventura County
Danny Orozco, Classroom Teacher
Luzmaria Espinosa, Poet-Teacher

90's Rock & Roll Lover

I'm a rock and roll lover.
I'm gonna live my life like there's no other.
I'm gonna stand tall and never back down.
I'm a 90's rocker and you can't put me down.
Living on the edge, pushing my limit,
the rush of adrenaline coursing through my veins.
Cruising down the highway, my hair in the wind,
I'm ready for anything I'm ready to begin.
I'm a rebel, a fighter, a rock and roll lover.
I'm gonna live my life because there is no other.
I'm gonna stand tall and not back down.
I'm a 90's lover and you will never put me down.
Guitar in my hand and heart on my sleeve,
I'm singing my heart out and I won't ever leave.
Playing with love and singing with soul.
Crowds going wild because I'm playing like a true rock
child.
I'm a rebel, a fighter, a rock and roll lover,
living my life like there is no tomorrow.
I'm standing tall and never looking back.
I'm a 90's rock and roll lover and I ain't ever getting put
down.
Keep on rockin 'till the end of times,
I'll never give in, I'll never resign.
Keep on singing and playing my guitar.
I ain't letting anyone dim my star.

Fatima 'Rios' Mozo, Grade 10
Alliance Cindy & Bill Simon Tech High, Los Angeles County
Anna Benavides, Classroom Teacher
Juan Cardenas, Poet-Teacher

Seventeen

I am seventeen years old
And I know nothing.

I enter, blind, into this Jungle called adulthood
this silent, glistening Sea called progress.
I know nothing of sealed fates, of the
world's weight: I wait not
for things to come. I create them.

In this Great Tide Pool called society,
I am the white foam atop a rising wave —
my generation rising with me.

We turn not to the pallid glow of the
lighthouse: how's light to guide us when
we have for centuries been
through the ebb and flow?

Indeed, you know me
You have dreamed the same dream,
eyes shone with that gleam,
felt the same spirit
of seventeen.

But in this moment, it is our turn:
We race toward a tomorrow not better, but worse
Our waves carry your sorrow through conditions adverse
And still, we will create

Our shining eyes look out on a gray horizon
We lift our anchor, prepare to rise and —
From it, we will create

Seventeen may be a number
But we are not too young for wonder,
And knowing, knowing our word's weight:

We must, and we will, create.

Amy Liu, Grade 12
Developing Virtue Girls School, Mendocino County
Jin Jr Shi, Classroom Teacher
Blake More, Poet-Teacher

You Asked What It Is To Be

A Letter About A Withering Painter

To my dearest stars,

Vincent is painting yet again.
The brush is trembling in his grip,
like the earthquake rumbling in his ribs.
Tonight, we are his muse.

He is reflecting on the melancholy yellow,
and how it stuck to his tongue like melted taffy.
The wind is singing its siren song,
swaying with the ocean waves.
We know it calls to him,
reaching into his heart to ease the quake.

Fame is in fate's palm;
we feel its power in the air.
The town is quiet on this night,
its warmth, a low buzz in the floor,
like the electricity in their lamps.

You are out of touch, my stars.
Your visibility is limited, hiding deep in the night
like a secret lingering on a pair of lips.
Even then, he continues to capture your beauty,
quick strokes of understanding blues and whispered yellows.

If only he knew how much love he will receive -
if he could feel the thrum of it in his chest,
like the beating heart of mother earth.

With adoration and worry,
Your beloved moon

Trinity Holm, Grade 11
Bear River High School, Nevada County
Kristina Stroeve, Classroom Teacher
Kirsten Casey, Poet-Teacher

A Star In The Abyss

I'm a shining star, floating in the quantum abyss.
I'm a faraway planet, so close, yet so far away.
I'm bigger than Pluto, but nothing can see me.
I'm just a tiny planet in a huge universe.
I do good things, but no one seems to care.
I have good things, but I don't deserve them.
If something happens to me, no one cares.
I'm in a galaxy that no one can see.
Sometimes, I feel like no one cares about me.
I just feel like a Star In The Abyss.

Jude Hagy, Grade 3
Francis Scott Key Elementary School, San Francisco County
Sarah Chan, Classroom Teacher
Susan Terence, Poet-Teacher

I Am The Universe

I am the fire of a horse
that will never burn out,
that stays throughout life
I am the loyalty of a wolf
to its family,
yet has the strength
to walk alone
I am the light of a candle
never to go out
until I melt
I am the stars in the sky
leading a herd, a pack
or a lonely traveler,
a star to call a friend
or support in the darkest hours
I am the raging wildfire
that lights when angered
by heat and wind
I am a barn owl
who is silent, yet wise
calm, yet ready to strike
I am a child
led by the Father
and spreading a message
I am a land in your head
with comforting sights
I am the wind

that follows a path,
a hawk soaring overhead
I am night with constellations
and the moon and stars
rising with wonder
a feather dancing in the wind
or a book with a wondrous adventure

I am the universe
you call home!

Kayleigh Estrada, Grade 6
John B. Riebli Elementary School, Sonoma County
Jacklyn Zagacki, Classroom Teacher
Michele Krueger, Poet-Teacher

Chameleon

From the prehistoric slime whence we came, here we stand.
'Midst our technologies and advancements,
we have built a world of our own design.
Science and literature define us, and through our
enlightenment,
what we do not understand must, indeed, harm us.

We fear what we cannot comprehend,
and thus, categorize everything.
We put things, people, in boxes,
label them with or without consent.
What they do not see, what they fail to recognize:
no one is black or white.
We crooked trees do not fit into your mills.

So here I stand. Unholy.
Abandoned by god, cast out from the order that bound me.
In my freedom, I face the fury of all those
who don't care to understand.
In my freedom, however, I am like a chameleon.
I am who I choose to be.
The binds that controlled me have released,
and thus, my ever-changing form may finally be.

Percival, Anton, Rasputin, Kevyan, Elna, Ray.

Though our world is built in resolute conformity, and rigidity,
I will bite the hands that feed me, and find my own food.

Parker Vassel, Grade 12
East High School, Humboldt County
Scott Betts, Classroom Teacher
Dan Zev Levinson, Poet-Teacher

Why Me?

I watch the sugar boiling down
The scents of the kitchen swirling around
Snails on plates
Quail tails on platters
1000's of brothers and sisters of mine
I hope I'm savory
Eaten by someone good
Not split with a cat like Amelia
Shared with a dog like Bedelia
No half-price like Jenni
No knife advertisements like Jacky
Okay, here's what I'm really thinking:
WHY ME!?!?!?!?!?!?!?!

Danica Alber-Silverstein, Grade 3
Kid Street Charter School, Sonoma County
Maris Talaugon, Classroom Teacher
Sandra Anfang, Poet-Teacher

I Am

I am scared,
tired
I have sorrow, my heart with a big barrow
I am ready, dismissing thoughts,
Sins in my hand I did not want to say,
Dragons I do not want to slay
I am Powerful, unstopped, Nothing
in my way, that will Break
apart my Play!
I stand my ground. Here.

Perla Sanchez, Grade 4
Vieja Valley Elementary School, Santa Barbara County
Tairy Birkley, Classroom Teacher
Cie Gumucio, Poet-Teacher

Meow

Sand,
I'm sorry if I scare you when I trample down the stairs
When you ran to the couch, I felt tears brim in my eyes
I wish I could take back everything I did
But I cannot, only, why?
I remember the first time I held you in my arms
I knew you were the perfect match for me
In a hat, asleep, Meow
But now that bond is broken
I see the way you crawl up on my parents' chests
And not mine
I'm sorry, Sand, for all I did
I wish to you the best of Meow

Danica Alber-Silverstein, Grade 3
Kid Street Charter School, Sonoma County
Maris Talaugon, Classroom Teacher
Sandra Anfang, Poet-Teacher

Be Calm

Dear Vincent,
the image projected inside, as if captured
on a freshly built camera,
is not a replica of the world.
brushstrokes on my head
comb my hair,
like a mother on her child's wedding day.
i urge you to be calm, like the waves after a storm.
the paints and i, hand in hand, are like a welded arc.
taste them like a good meal,
feel them like a warm summer breeze,
hear them like a story seen only in your head.
i urge you to be calm.

XOXO,
Paintbrush

Gabby Gerster, Grade 11
Bear River High School, Nevada County
Kristina Stroeve, Classroom Teacher
Kirsten Casey, Poet-Teacher

The Baseball

I am a baseball.
I am playing in my first game ever.
How exciting!
I am looking at the batter,
nervous about what is going to happen.
I am about to be thrown and then,
Bam!
I am thrown at 66 miles per hour.
I feel so alive,
the wind hitting my face.
Then, I'm hit by the baseball bat.
I feel the pain.
After a few seconds, it goes away.
I land on the green grass.
I am picked up by a random guy.
I say to myself,
Could this man be famous?
I stop and focus.
I am thrown again.
In the air, I'm on my way to meet a new guy.
That man is shortstop.
He throws me to a man in a lot of gear.
I land in his glove,
which was very tight,
and then I smack into the runner's leg.
A man in a mask says,
You're out!

I am disappointed because I got someone out,
but everyone starts cheering.
I guess I did do something good after all.
Let's finish this game, shall we?

Vincent Ruckrigl, Grade 6
Willowside Middle School, Sonoma County
Nicola Niedermair, Classroom Teacher
Brennan DeFrisco, Poet-Teacher

Why Me?

I am the book
that you make use of too much.
You thrust me into the depths of your backpack
like I am the crumb,
sitting deep beside a bitten pencil.
I am frantic
thinking about you taking me out at lunch.
My cover,
frayed with scratches,
ready to be scratched more
by various hands.
Did you know
that it hurts to be withdrawn,
like the paper of notes
stuffed down beside
the isolated pen?
Did you ever think
that it stings to be thrown,
like a bundle of sharp razors?
Have you ever
felt the agony
of someone bending a part of you back,
like you're not even there
just to save something they want
later in life?
Why me?, I ask.
When one has so many books as you,
Why me?

Ever since my pages were stamped into my seam,
I knew life would be vigorous.
However, you bought me a little exultation
through the long years one has—
the way you gaze into my cover,
after reading me for the 100th time.
I feel pride you can only feel once.
It makes me feel gratitude
for the writer who is responsible,
for picking up their hands
full of story,
imagination,
and beginning to write.
Even though you have done an abundance
of things wrong,
I know you mean well.
You just want to rejoice in reading me.

Olivia Forget, Grade 6
Willowside Middle School, Sonoma Country
Nicola Niedermair, Classroom Teacher
Brennan DeFrisco, Poet-Teacher

Pencil Personification

I first remember being sealed in a box
A box devoid of life
A box filled with others of my kind.
1 by 1, the others were seized, unfortunately:
Jimmy, Oscar, Timothy.
Picked up by a giant with "limbs" protruding from his body.
I heard they are called "legs" and "arms."
Eventually, I was picked up by the giant.
He carried me to a different box,
only this box had a metal blade.
He stuck me in and spun me around,
exposing the graphite that was inside of me.
He exposed it by shaving off my skin.
After the anguish of what happened faded,
I mistakenly thought it was over,
but then he smeared my graphite all over paper.
He continued to smear my graphite,
then he did the unthinkable: he flipped me around
using my eraser to get rid of my graphite.
All the agony for nothing. I was fuming.
I was eternally grateful when I shrunk, too small to be used.
The torture was over,
finally.

Skyler Freedenburg, Grade 6
Willowside Middle School, Sonoma County
Nicola Niedermair, Classroom Teacher
Brennan DeFrisco, Poet-Teacher

I Am A Trash Bin

I am a trash bin –
unwanted,
unloved,
disrespected,
replaced by Compost, Recycle, and even TerraCycle,
although they're just different labels.
You sometimes use me as a makeshift basketball hoop.
I flinch every time you miss.
You say my contents fill the oceans,
but I am just a name to blame.
You fill me with paper unworthy of
a great story, a letter, a poem.
The thin crumpled paper in me was once capable
of great things.
I'm just a plastic coffin,
holding the corpse of your mistakes.
My traveling is limited to bare and boring classrooms.
Each kid squeaks,
a scream in my ears.
Next time, thank me after I do you a simple favor.
Next time, think about being choked down with "trash."
Next time, give a smile on your way out.
because I'll be here forever.

Joseph Gannon, Grade 6
Willowside Middle School, Sonoma County
Nicola Niedermair, Classroom Teacher
Brennan DeFrisco, Poet-Teacher

Lion of the Rainbow

I am the lion of the rainbow.
I learn to hunt like a wolf.
I taught the sun to burn the rain.
I dream of cheetahs running
like the wind.

Jack Gorman, Kindergarten
Alexander Valley School, Sonoma County
Julie Axell, Classroom Teacher
Maureen Hurley, Poet-Teacher

The Lemur

My bushy tail keeps me steady
as I walk around the long forest branches,
yelling to call a meeting.
Gathered and cuddled together tightly
as the wind blows harshly,
I try to sleep as my mother squeezes me.
I wake up and see it's morning,
other lemurs eating quickly,
yelling and screaming,
trying to communicate with each other.
Walking and jumping, I do.
Still trying to stay steady:
my ancestors, old and gray,
but they're lively and love to play.
Through the plants and trees,
curious and excited I am,
long days are going by fast.
Challenging and scary,
many adventures ahead of me.
Leaping onto other lemurs' heads,
and getting smarter,
knowing I'm small,
I will soon be as big as my big, lively heart.

Nora Bottari, Grade 4
Prestwood Elementary School, Sonoma County
Nichole Roberts, Classroom Teacher
Sandra Anfang, Poet-Teacher

I Am the Island Night Lizard

I am the island night lizard.
I am the sandy diamond island night lizard,
crawling in the northern lights.

I wish I were the minty silver sage, growing
in the wind.
No one knows I am really a spiky crystal
book, flapping.

I am the crystal sap inside the island night
lizard, waiting to emerge. How will I ever
come out of this black hole?

Sometimes, I feel like the scared octopus,
hiding. Being that way is no way to live.

Silas Yee, Grade 5
West Portal Elementary School, San Francisco County
Kathleen Schick, Classroom Teacher
Susan Terence, Poet-Teacher

Dear Mother,

You asked what it is to be in the mine.
It is as tangible to breath as drowning
in a mug of beer: deep, earthy and thick.
One that tastes of dirt and sourgrass,
one of earthworm compost and mud.
It is darkness as tight as a giant serpent,
belly pressed against the walls,
wrapped thick leather scales and packed full.
We wonder if we, too, are the rats inside its gut
as we squeeze past the suffocating organs
and blood-pumped darkness.

It is to see flowers of Sweet Anne's lace,
glowing as visible as dust in the sun,
as real as thin air is to blind eyes:
visible and absent.
Callused, dirt-lined fingers, tough as obsidian,
lit by a single twisting flame,
glimmering like Tommy Knockers
dancing deep in the gold lined tunnels.

Warm, like sunbaked Himalayan blackberries,
each fruit glowing with internal heat from its core.
Now, turned cold in tin lunch boxes.
Sunday foraging scratches,
once fresh and stinging with blood and juice,
now turned faint scars,
dusty, like hairline cracks in stone

Sophie Conner, Grade 11
Sierra Academy of Expeditionary Learning, Nevada County
Marika Beck, Classroom Teacher
Kirsten Casey, Poet-Teacher

I Am A Man

I am a man of great honor
A man of my word and my sword
A man who carries the stars on his shoulder
and the stains of red on his back

I am a man of Liao
A man whose victories are known by many
A man whose homeland calls him a hero
I am a man, strong and true,
with a heart that beats for all I do

I am a man of the battlefield
A man who knows it all
The lingering taste of fear
The feeling of disappointment
The screams of tragedy and pain
The sight of death happening right before my eyes
I am a man who knows it all too well

I am a man of sorrow
A man who's unable to let go
A man who carries burden upon burden
My responsibilities
My troubles
Pile on and on

I am a man who yearns for change
If I was a cleverer man

A smart man like my father
A tough man like my brothers
A better man like my uncles
The best man there was
I could be happier

I am a man of many strengths
I have so much to offer
My bravery in the face of danger
My dedication to my job and lords
My independence from leaving home young
And yet
I am my own weakness,
my own downfall

I am a man

Kaela Liao, Grade 9
Lowell High School, San Francisco County
Jacqueline Moses, Classroom Teacher
Susan Terence, Poet-Teacher

My Transformation

I am a butterfly.
I once was a wormlike creature.
I once squirmed like a legless child.
I then went into a deathlike doze.
I rose out of my doze, twenty-one subsequent solar days.
I then became a soaring creature.
I now flutter through the spring breeze.
I am now an aqua blue, like a spring's stream.
I have white rings on my wings, like clouds on an aqua sky.
I do not like bees.
I have a weakness for magnolias.
If I were to say, I am pleasing to look at.
I am a butterfly.

Trinity Miller, Grade 9
McKinleyville High School, Humboldt County
Karen Myers and Jessica Raymer, Classroom Teachers
Dan Zev Levinson, Poet-Teacher

Mother Nature

I am a citrine fox, tricky and sly
I am a towering, stiff redwood tree
never backing down
I live with the stars and nebulas
The space air tastes smoky and bitter
I am a tilapia fleeing from a shark, weaving
through the bright coral
I am on a hill
The blazing sun turns me into a hot tomato
I am a calm cow fat and happy but the farmer
needs a burger
I run through the silky grass
With nature I feel fuller than ever before

Vincent Ko, Grade 5
West Portal Elementary School, San Francisco County
Kathleen Schick, Classroom Teacher
Susan Terence, Poet-Teacher

A Mysterious Predator

Swooping through air, snatching my prey,
Catching the wind on a bright, breezy, day.
Looking for food, either rotten or fresh,
Feeding my babies, and seeing red flesh.
I swoop and I glide, winding through trees
Watch my family eat, then devour the rest.
I'm a carnivore, sorry, I only eat meat,
No animal eats me so I'm not a treat.
The rabbits I chase if I cannot find fish,
live near the garden, eat beets and other healthy treats.
I have laws to protect me so humans can't hunt,
I'm a symbol of peace in America.
What mysterious creature am I?
Why I'm the great bald eagle, of course!

Emily Price-Braschler, Grade 3
Prestwood Elementary School, Sonoma County
Gwen Watson, Classroom Teacher
Sandra Anfang, Poet-Teacher

The Golden Eagle

I am seen as the tiny white cloud
Always overshadowed by the storm
Wishing I had another job.
No one knows who I really am,
The Golden Eagle,
Soaring
Am I not proud?
Sometimes, I feel no one thinks so.

Adrian Zarate-Sanderlin, Grade 5
West Portal Elementary School, San Francisco County
Kathleen Schick, Classroom Teacher
Susan Terence, Poet-Teacher

Above The World

I am a Peregrine Falcon
Soaring over the forest ground
I smell the misty clouds
I taste the sprinkled drops
I feel the wind blasting
through my feathers
I hear the river raging below me
I see and hear you
Jettisoning your trash
All over our earth
Will you stop clouding up our skies
with your tall, tall smoke stacks
Stop polluting our seas
Everyone deserves to fly

Max O Post-Leib, Grade 6
Manchester School, Mendocino County
Amy Ruegg, Classroom Teacher
Blake More, Poet-Teacher

The Feather

I am a feather.
Watch as I fall off my bird.

I float in the wind
I feel forgotten.
People can pick me up and toss me
back on the ground.

thump
There I go again
when I fall to the ground
for the very last time.
I forget to love myself.

I wish I was the ocean,
big and strong,
fearless and crystal blue,
loved by all.

There is a story in every wave,
you can lose your thoughts
by the sound of a crash,
like a story waiting to unfold.

I am a feather

but, I am the ocean
inside.

Sorcha B. Fornara, Grade 4
Montecito Union School, Santa Barbara County
Barbara Gonzales, Classroom Teacher
Cie Gumucio, Poet-Teacher

I Am the Ocean

I am the ocean,
blue as the biggest whale

I am the monkey,
climbing the trees

I am the backpack
that holds your books.

I am the notebook
that you write on.

I am the pencil
that you write with.

I am the watch
that tells time.

I am the dancer,
tapping on the stage
I am the dog
that goes bark-bark.

I am the soap
that you use
to wash your hands.

I am the chair
that you sit on.

Joel Pierce, Grade 3
Logan Memorial Educational Campus, San Diego County
Alexis Carney, Classroom Teacher
Johnnierenee Nia Nelson, Poet-Teacher

Violet Blue

I live in the bottom of the ocean.
I move gracefully, but fast.
My house is made out of seashells.
I was born during the winter on New Years.
I love to swim and dance all around.
I am afraid of humans and large sharks.
My shirt is made out of seashells.
My pants are made out of seaweed.
My favorite food is clams and lobsters.
My favorite sound is crash.
I wish I was like my mom, a beautiful octopus.
My heart is a firework exploding.

Chloe Confiac, Grade 4
Mountain View Elementary School, Santa Barbara County
Carly Schmiess, Classroom Teacher
Cie Gumucio, Poet-Teacher

Fire's Point of View

I am Fire
Outspoken
Underrated
Skipped over
Put out

I am almost always misunderstood
Only a few people understand and accept me
Only a few appreciate me
I'm only so often given a voice to speak with
Very few respect me as who I am
Those who do, I share the same thoughts and feelings

Embers keep me company
They allow me to spread, so I'm known
They make me feel a warmth that I didn't know was possible

With the cost of the trees and grass,
I see them as both my friends and my rivals
I'm called rude and destructive
I don't get a say in anything, except what burns

Thank you for letting me speak.

Jenevieve Shaw, Grade 6
Willowside Middle School, Sonoma County
Nicola Niedermair, Classroom Teacher
Brennan DeFrisco, Poet-Teacher

Dear God

My burden weighs me down
like an oversaturated cloud
too heavy for me to carry
and it rains down on me.
The sky is infuriatingly silent,
like the breath before a sob.
The taste of it, like dust,
wasted away by a downpour.
I bite my tongue
and the blood lingers there, metallic,
like the earth itself is rooted in my mouth.
What did I do to deserve this
heaviness?
It devastates me.
I am empty, poured out
like a glass strung with cobwebs.

Yours forever,

Vincent

Jude Slater, Grade 11
Bear River High School, Nevada County
Kristina Stroeve, Classroom Teacher
Kirsten Casey, Poet-Teacher

I Am

I am the aqua hours
I am a dog running through the sky
I am a vibrant blue piano
I am the song that swims through your ears
I am the wind that rushes through your hair
I am nature running through the night
I am the great sadness and happiness
I am the thing you come to talk to
I am a harmless spider
I am the wow in the world
I am the dream you see
I am old as the very beginning
I am also as young as the coming
I am time itself
I am millions of books swirling around in a storm
I am billions of raindrops falling on the world's crust
I am my brother's burdens
I am my mother's sorrows
I am my grandma's spirit
I stand on top of the world
    You know I am with you
        with you

Renee Stehmeier, Grade 4
Vieja Valley Elementary School, Santa Barbara County
Kirk Reeves, Classroom Teacher
Cie Gumucio, Poet-Teacher

Who Feeds Me Joy & Happiness

In Praise of Mama

after Maybe I'm Amazed by The Beatles

Maybe it's the way you love me all the time.
Maybe I'm amazed at the way you sing to me at night.
Maybe it's the way I really need you.
Maybe I'm amazed at the way you remind me I can do it.
Maybe it's the way you make our house a home.
Maybe I'm amazed at the way you right me when I'm wrong.
Maybe it's the way you put me on the right path.
Maybe I'm amazed at the way you walk me to school.
Maybe it's the way you help me feel better.
Maybe I'm amazed at the way you have always loved me.
Maybe it's the way you help me sing my song.

Maybe it's all these things that make you so amazingly awesome.
Maybe I'm amazed at the way I love you.

Abigail Hall, Grade 3
Mountain View Elementary School, Santa Barbara County
Pia Tsuruda, Classroom Teacher
Cie Gumucio, Poet-Teacher

My Mom

Who remembers everything
Whose eyes are brown as copper
In her, I see a sea of kindness
Whose hands are smooth like opals
Whose voice is like a cloud
She is a red fox, running
She is a tower, tall and strong
She gives me a home
A place to feel welcome
I want to give you a story
of red, white, and blue dragons
soaring in the night sky.
For you, a tale of heartfelt winters in the valley.
Here is a song of orange and yellow leaves
falling off of the trees, swaying in the wind.
Dance with the woodland animals
Watching the fading sunset
yet, illuminating the world.
Surround yourself in the sea of loved ones.
Taste the fresh air.
Hear the breeze embrace the world.

Rhys Burkhart, Grade 5
West Portal Elementary School, San Francisco County
Marina DeGroot, Classroom Teacher
Susan Terence, Poet-Teacher

Ode To Mother Nature

You are so magnificent
You fill me with awe
Serene as a mountain stream
Beautiful as a peacock
Wise as an owl
A home for all

You are so amazing
you fill my heart with hope
Your courageous spirit
as bold as a star in the sky

How can you be so optimistic
when we are killing you as I write?

You are the brightest thing in space
Radiating life
Your kindness is like a golden dove,
Dominating all existence

Mabel Carpenter, Grade 3
Tamalpais Valley School, Marin County
Karen Croy, Classroom Teacher
Michele Rivers, Poet-Teacher

An Ode to Orcas

Oh, Orca! Oh, Orca!
How are you dark, but also, light?
Even the shark bows before thy might!
Your wing-like fins power you through the water.
Is this because you are the ocean's daughter?

Oh, human. Oh, child.
Let me teach you a thing about being wild,
'Cause life and death and in between
Will punish you if you are mean.
But if you are nice and kind,
You can enter an orca's mind.

Caleb Taboada, Grade 4
Park School, Marin County
Leslie Bernstein, Classroom Teacher
Claire Blotter, Poet-Teacher

Ode to Beautiful Blue Waters

Oh, teal waves crashing onto silvery rocks
Oh, shimmery liquid that shines through the sunset
Do you know how much we honor your moving sounds?
Why do you make scary, giant noises?
Have you ever thought about taking a calm break?
You are like bright sunshine
You are mysterious and fierce
You kind to all creatures
You smell like green seaweed
You look like rain sprinkling in wind
You taste like sweet white salt
You feel like smooth, soft foam
You sound like two cats fighting each other
Thank you for letting us swim in you

Melissa Cienega, Grade 4
Manchester School, Mendocino County
Avis Anderson, Classroom Teacher
Blake More, Poet-Teacher

Her

If she were to carry Medusa's curse
I would stare into her eyes and let my stone body
gaze at Her perfection for eternity.

If God were to give me eternal life,
I would turn it down because a life without Her
is no different than death itself.

And if she had as many tears as there are drops in the sea,
I would spend my last breath drowning in Her sorrow.

Joshua Raygoza, Grade 10
Alliance Cindy & Bill Simon Tech High, Los Angeles County
Anna Benavides, Classroom Teacher
Juan Cardenas, Poet-Teacher

My Baba

Who is from the mountains of heaven
Who calls me Ljubavi
Who tells me how beautiful I am every single day
Whose eyes are like the crystal waters of Croatia
In her, I see the fighter never giving up
Whose hands are like a tiger
working hard for its food
Who feeds me joy and happiness
Whose voice is like a song that never ends
She is like a sweet, loving elephant
She gives me life
I thank her for everything
She is the reason that I am happy
to come home every day
I would tell her, "You are beautiful," every single day
I would give her the world

Lola Finci, Grade 5
West Portal Elementary School, San Francisco County
Kathleen Schick, Classroom Teacher
Susan Terence, Poet-Teacher

My Friend, Maggie

Who is from China
Who calls me Yuelin,
Who tells me all about herself
Who remembers the good times we had
    when we were in 2nd grade
Whose eyes are dark brown, like a stone
Whose hands are strong, like a tree
Who feeds me confidence
Who voice is like the sweet scent of a rose
She has the heart of a wild jaguar
She gives me hope and confidence
In her, I see confidence in her eyes
I thank her for all the things she has done
She is the reason that I can't wait to come to school every day
I would tell her thank you every day
I would give her hope and company everyday

Yuelin Zhou, Grade 3
Francis Scott Key Elementary School, San Francisco County
Ryan Van Arkel, Classroom Teacher
Susan Terence, Poet-Teacher

My Best Friend Yuelin

Who was born in California
Who calls me Maggie
Who tells me every funny thing that happened at her house
Who remembers all the great times we had since second grade!
Whose eyes are wise as the dragons
Whose hands are as fierce as the tigers
Who gives me hope
Whose voice can be as loud as thunder
I see the happy, blue skies and calm clouds within her
She is a hope, even in the toughest of times
She is a drum with the loudest beats
She gives me the encouragement to try things
      I never had before
I thank her for helping me even in the loneliest times
She is the reason for all the jokes and riddles I tell others
I would tell her that she was one of the first
      and best friends I ever had!
I would give her the exact support she has given me.

Minzhi Huang, Grade 3
Francis Scott Key Elementary School, San Francisco County
Ryan Van Arkel, Classroom Teacher
Susan Terence, Poet-Teacher

A La Que Me Dio La Vida

A la que me dio la vida:
gran mujer trabajadora,
tus creaciones afloran
en el amor de tu niña.
Conexiones femeninas,
diferencias, hay unas;
reflejamos como lunas.
Siempre vivirás en mí;
sin ti no pudo existir
tú y yo como almas juntas.

Carla Orta, Grade 10
Watsonville High School, Santa Cruz County
Juan Carlos Pozo Block, Classroom Teacher
Bob Gómez, Poet-Teacher

My Dad

Who is from Colorado
Who calls me, "Dill Pickle"
Who tells me to stop being such
    "a big dill"
Who remembers everything in my life
Whose eyes are blue and full of color
In him, I see happiness and mountains
    of color
Whose hands are chilly
Who feeds me excellent
warm grilled cheeses
Whose voice is deep and high
He is a green frog, happily hopping
He is a guitar, running
He gives me lollipops
I thank him for his love and joy
I would tell him he makes me feel special
I would give him the world

Dylan Hylton, Grade 5
West Portal Elementary School, San Francisco County
Kathleen Schick, Classroom Teacher
Susan Terence, Poet-Teacher

My Papa and My Mama

My papa
Who is from the land of the first people.
Who calls me Alaji.
Who tells me stories of his home when I'm sad.
Who remembers when I was the only kid around.
Whose eyes are a deep brown sea.
Whose hands could hold the earth.
Who feeds me joy and knowledge.
Whose voice is as deep as the Atlantic.
In him, I see big, kind, towering mountains
just like him. He is my papa.

My mama
Who is from the land of 10,000 lakes.
Who gives me confidence on stage and at home.
Who remembers my first seconds of life.
Whose eyes are as green as the leaves
of the redwood tree in the backyard.
Whose hands provide shelter and protection
In her, I see a lion protecting its cubs.
Who feeds me joy and bravery. She is my mom.

Alaji Sey, Grade 5
Longfellow Elementary School, San Francisco County
Sheryl Carrillo, Classroom Teacher,
Susan Terence, Poet-Teacher

Ode to Shoes

Oh, shoes.
All would be hopeless without you.
Your gorgeous hues of emerald green,
Your silky, long laces, holding you on my feet.
Oh shoes,
Your lovely physique matches my feet perfectly.
Most may think you are normal, average.
But back when Hermes' caduceus guided people to the afterlife,
    you were rare.
Oh shoes,
Back then, no pair, not even Theseus' sandals,
    were as good as you.
Now, no one appreciates a good pair of shoes.
Oh shoes,
You are like armor in battle, shields for my feet.
Without you, every step would be torture.
Oh shoes,
It would feel like nonstop migraines, head pounding,
Wonderful thoughts barricaded by my mind throbbing,
My cranium pulsing.
Oh shoes,
I am honored, truly honored,
that you choose to wear me.

Nolan Perry, Grade 6
Willowside Middle School, Sonoma County
Nicola Niedermair, Classroom Teacher
Brennan DeFrisco, Poet-Teacher

Dear Joy

You are my playful puppy, licking peanut butter off my face.
You are my goat, eating paper for a snack.
You are the spark in the stars during a full moon.
You are the happy ripples of life when my best friends
        make me laugh so hard, I fall off my chair.
You are each music note every time my brother and I sing
        'til we are so tired, we can't move a bone.
You are my goats, Dandelion and Poppy
Cloppity clop, when I take them on walks
You are the sun shining when I get up in the morning
You're my bunny, who thinks she's a queen.
I look forward to you every day.

Thank you, joy!

Abby Gelfand, Grade 4
Strawberry Point School, Marin County
Lulu Monti, Classroom Teacher
Terri Glass, Poet-Teacher

Thanksgiving

Oh, it is Thanksgiving!
So many helping hands.
When the air is filled with the smell of gravy,
this forgiving feast begins.
The turkey shimmers, like a smile.
The gravy splatters on my plate, like a waterfall.
Mmmmmm,
So savory.
Glad you like it, my mom softly murmurs.
When I look deep into the candlelight,
I can see my thanks is sent out to the world.
I think about the store workers
who helped stock the gravy
The truck drivers who drive for miles
The farmers who harvested the broccoli.
Like that, I am finished with dinner.
I go to the hand-carved bar stools
and look at the shimmering apple crumble.
I take a bite.
I love my auntie's cooking
because she makes the best mashed potatoes
and the best rice.
And that's why I love Thanksgiving.

Felix Wilmarth, Grade 3
Kid Street Charter School, Sonoma County
Maris Talaugon, Classroom Teacher
Sandra Anfang, Poet-Teacher

Happiness

Joy is laying in the cool summer grass
as the sun shines on me
and watching the blue birds
fly with the golden sun on their wings

Joy is playing tag on the shimmering ground
with my friends and going down the fast slide

Joy is like skiing down the sparkling mountain
with the wind whipping against my face and the
sound of my skis sliding against the snow

Joy is eating juicy corn dogs and
cheese pizza that stretches apart
it's so delicious

Joy is me because I am full of happiness every day
Are you?

Griffin Martino, Grade 2
Nicasio School, Marin County
Ellian Klein, Classroom Teacher
Michele Rivers, Poet-Teacher

Love Me and All My Imperfections

Love me and all my imperfections
Love me when I am dancing like no one is watching
Love me when I stuff my face with my favorite food
Love me when I am crying over a movie
that just hit too close home
Love me when all I can do is talk and talk without stopping
Love me when I had a bad day and I want to do is sleep
Love me when I feel insecure
Love me when my wounds are out and I am vulnerable to
anything around me—

Love me, love me, love me

Love me with all that I am
Love me with all that I am
Love what you know and what you see within me
Every single scar, mole, smile, tear, frown
All of it

Love me and all my imperfections.

Sofia Noriega, Grade 10
Oxnard Middle College High School, Ventura County
Kim Stephenson, Classroom Teacher
Angelina Leaños, Poet-Teacher

Nature's Music

The Wilderness in Me

There is an octopus living inside me,
a strange, majestic, magical swimmer.

It taught me to be me and block any opinions out
with inkful proudness and how to escape
to a safe place of music.
 The Wilderness left it for me in the coral reef.

There is a horse living inside me, a dirty
but beautiful creature.

It taught me to calm down and not care
what others think of me and just trot by them
and get to live life happily.
 The Wilderness left it for me in a beautiful field.

There is a California condor living inside me,
a giant, strong, fearless bird.

It taught me to not be afraid and soar through fear.
 The Wilderness left it for me in a cloud.

Anson von Staden, Grade 4
Mountain View Elementary School, Santa Barbara County
Katherine James, Classroom Teacher
Cie Gumucio, Poet-Teacher

Last Night The Rain Spoke To Me

after Mary Oliver

Last night the rain
spoke to me.
It said,
I'm so happy
to be out of a cloud!
I love the rain
because
it feels
amazing.
I feel
comfortable.
I'm
home.

Natalia Martins, Grade 3
Chenoweth Elementary School, Merced County
Meuy Saeteurn, Classroom Teacher
Dawn Trook, Poet-Teacher

A Watery World

after a painting by Jess Collins

A rainbow of rain,
A fountain of colors,
A mirror only I can see,
Fields of money,
Flowers full of love,
Colors that don't exist.

One light, a circle
of laughter and joy,
Excitement that is overflowing.
It feels like the ends
of the earth.

Until a dark shadow,
A figure of no sort,
has eyes in the back
of his head,
shuffling cards,
fingers like a witch.
Show yourself.

It feels like a whisper,
A key with no lock,
Or a lock with no key,
A mystery like a sad song
with no end.

A rainbow of rain.

A shadow upon them.
Hoot, hoot, whispers the owl.
Raindrops like a mountain
of color, like a mirror
only I can see.
Everything slipping
far away

far away.
A river of color.

Izzy Kirke, Grade 4
Park School, Marin County
Leslie Bernstein, Classroom Teacher
Claire Blotter, Poet-Teacher

Anna's Hummingbird

The hummingbird hovered, then landed on the glass blown feeder
and I thought about this magnificent, beautiful creature:
As shiny as a pearl and as smooth as marble.
In bright, iridescent green, with a throat as bright as a pink
shooting star. So beautiful, yet so delicate, as it turns into
the sun with movements like a lightning bolt.
It has soft, velvety, white down underneath its fanlike crescent
moon. Tail now folded into two flat, straight, green boards.
It has a beak like a black needle, ready to drink up the liquid.
As it flies away, I see its beating wings as it hovers with its
head perfectly still, frozen in the air, then it suddenly flies far,
far away, zooming over the trees.

Everett Heller, Grade 5
Strawberry Point School, Marin County
Rachel Quek, Classroom Teacher
Terri Glass, Poet-Teacher

Dance the Pomegranate

Dance the pomegranate, sweetness to savor,
like grenades of juice, bursting with flavor.
A room of excitement, a room of seeds,
soft and chewable, fitting your needs.
Dance the pomegranate, and you shall seek
the flavor of flavors, soon to leak
from your mouth and onto your shirt
not too easy, this juice is too clean.
Now go on, go on, buy a few
the fruit of heaven, the fruit for you.

Cortland Gamble, Grade 5
Strawberry Point School, Marin County
Daniel Gasparini, Classroom Teacher
Terri Glass, Poet-Teacher

Meadow

Walking through brown and yellow,
tall purple grains, like rough string,
my hands feeling it, listening to it,
venturing into it like a path to freedom,
collecting blackberries and small currants,
Cute, like little tasty jewels.
But though my hands are messy,
and my thumb bleeding from thorns,
I can still feel it, listen to it,
the tall, purple grains,
like rough string,
drinking the blood from my thumb.

Sophie Marvin, Grade 6
Fair Oaks School, Los Angeles County
Ericka Irwin, Classroom Teacher
Alice Pero, Poet-Teacher

To the Body of the Earth

To the body of the earth,
examined now, after the death
of your hidden cells and bones

Maybe the explosions felt like
the head of a pin piercing flesh
Hot and yellow after being pulled from a fire

Or maybe it was more of a quiet ache
like a rubber mallet on the
back of a soft old hand

Did you think it was worth it?
Providing
and feeding like a mother

dropping gold into rough open hands
Greed and hope spilling from men
like the rivers on your face

Your body feeding men
who feed you destruction in return
just to feed themselves

Dear body of the earth,
why are you generous to those
willing to pry?

Rewarding both the selfish and the selfless
who have no choice but to pick you away
No other choice

but to destroy beauty
with pupils dilated like black moons
and silver picks, like daggers in their hands

Josef Henry, Grade 11
Sierra Academy of Expeditionary Learning, Nevada County
Marika Beck, Classroom Teacher
Kirsten Casey, Poet-Teacher

Survival

How brave are the trees
who whisper in the breeze
as our world is burning

How brave are the animals
who drink from the streams
while we turn her rivers green

How brave is the ocean
who keeps crashing waves
as plastic is sitting polluting her

How brave is the ozone
who keeps protecting us
even while it's being torn apart

How brave is the world
who keeps spinning
even as we burn her and dam her rivers

Aurellia Boadecia, Grade 6
Orleans Elementary School, Humboldt County
Andie Butler-Crosby, Classroom Teacher
Dan Zev Levinson, Poet-Teacher

Voices From the Stars

I am a voice of change
whispering all the way
from the farthest stars.

We need to stop pollution,
for its fumes kill young animals.

We need to stop trash in the ocean,
for coral dies out.

We need to help the elderly,
and learn from our ancestors.

I am no longer a whisper,
now I am a shout.
We need our future to change,
so please hear me out.

Change is inside you,
change is inside everyone.
I am a voice of change
just like you.

Layla Conger, Grade 5
Cobb Elementary School, Lake County
Laurel Phillips, Classroom Teacher
Michele Krueger, Poet-Teacher

On the Other Side of the Ocean

On the other side of the ocean,
the great blue whale swims across the ocean, looking for food.

On the other side of the ocean,
dolphins come up above the waves to say, "squeak squeak!"

On the other side of the ocean,
The waves crash as the boat sails across the sea.

On the other side of the ocean,
Bright red crabs go pinch! pinch! at the bottom of the sea.

On the other side of the ocean,
The green sea turtle swims very fast.

The other side of the ocean is home.

Violet Shaw, Grade 3
Apple Blossom Elementary School, Sonoma County
Courtney Diedrich, Classroom Teacher
Lisa Shulman, Poet-Teacher

The Rain

The rain
The rain fell down
It looks like diamonds
It smells like a
balloon
It tastes like a ball
It feels wet
It Sounds like a sink full of
water
It makes me
feel calm
In the rain I jump in puddles
In the rain I feel a cold breeze
In the rain.

Sophia Dueñas, Grade 3
Chenoweth Elementary School, Merced County
Amy Brown, Classroom Teacher
Dawn Trook, Poet-Teacher

Peace

after Mary Oliver

Last night,
the rain spoke to me
Help me fall, it said,
so I fell with it
I fell in the pond
I fell deeper and deeper
Into the pond
I found it,
Peace,
but I found out that
it was with me
Inside me
Because I was with the rain
and the rain was with me

Alessandra Mensing, Grade 3
Chenoweth Elementary School, Merced County
Meuy Saeteurn, Classroom Teacher
Dawn Trook, Poet-Teacher

At Ease

you judge me
before you see
you don't know how it feels
to be at ease
up on the back of the horse
I feel like one
the breeze running through my hair
nothing compares
to the smell of dewy trees
blurs of brown and green
running past me
the sound of hooves on the ground

Georgia Emerson, Grade 6
Cobb Elementary School, Lake County
Laurel Phillips, Classroom Teacher
Michele Krueger, Poet-Teacher

All Alone

A snake wants to be a vine,
all alone and
nothing bothering it.

At night, all you see is a line,
green like the swamp it lives in.

Not wanting to be bothered—
yet, there isn't much to do
except to listen
to bickering and hollering.

Jose Fabian, Grade 7
Isbell Middle School, Ventura County
Danny Orozco, Classroom Teacher
Luzmaria Espinosa, Poet-Teacher

A Butterfly's Love

A butterfly is like a friend embracing,
hugging you with all her love.

It's like a puppy licking you
when your come back from a big trip.

A butterfly is a friend to ALL
and you, to a butterfly.

A butterfly is a star hugging
the moon. It's like a friend.

Eloise Wilson, Grade 2
Park School, Marin County
Sally Strike, Classroom Teacher
Claire Blotter, Poet-Teacher

Japanese Haiku

Misty mountain peaks
Covered in beautiful snow
Peaceful mountain tops

Red paper lanterns
Floating above koi filled ponds
Look like shining stars

Pink cherry blossoms
Guarding the gates to temples
The temple bell ring

Zoe Rogers, Grade 4
Lu Sutton Elementary School, Marin County
Pamela Stutzman, Classroom Teacher
Michele Rivers Poet-Teacher

The Snapdragon

The pink water lily taught me how to float
in the cool summer breeze.
The red snapdragon taught the purple Pride of Madeira,
how to dance in the sun.
The blue iris has secrets to tell you:
It can tell you that you can bloom anywhere in spring.
In the story of myself,
I hear words reading it.
I see pages being turned.
I feel a soft wind going over my head.

Simon Garvie, Grade 3
Francis Scott Key Elementary School, San Francisco County
Katherine Johnson, Classroom Teacher
Susan Terence, Poet-Teacher

The Flower In A Glass

Since the flower in the window
can be seen, but if it can't be seen,
it can't be loved
If it isn't loved, it will burn to nothingness
It wants to be nothing
because it can only be a flower in a glass
But still, the sun shines and the flower droops
like always, everything is the same forever
like the flower's sadness

Shiann Glushakow, Grade 6
Fair Oaks School, Los Angeles County
Ericka Irwin, Classroom Teacher
Alice Pero, Poet-Teacher

The Canary and The Crow

Bitter cold
That piles on windowsills
A sleeping city
As the sun settles in the hills

Inside
The renters and the owners
Apathy and awareness
Sympathetic blood donors

Clammy faces above chicken broth
Giggle and squeal
Under forts of cloth

Outside
The canary and the crow
Two body hearth
Amidst the whirling snow

The canary
Slow and sick with age
Fuel for men's curiosity
Fluttering poison gauge

The crow
Intentions misread
Disregarded
Has come to hate them like they said
The people

Through windows to the storm
Their indifference
Guards the secret of keeping warm

Cade Palmer, Grade 11
Marin School of the Arts, Novato High School, Marin County
Rebecca Pollack, Classroom Teacher
Maxine Flasher-Düzgüneş, Poet-Teacher

Fly Like a Bird

From the hills,
I learned to fly like a bird,
soaring, soaring in the sky,
with diamonds,
following behind me.

Abby Sheehy, Grade 2
Alexander Valley School, Sonoma County
Sarah Sheehy, Classroom Teacher
Maureen Hurley, Poet-Teacher

El Diluvio Del Pájaro 2023

Coro:
Deja de llorar
Deja de llorar
Que el diluvio del Pájaro que se desbordó
No te puede alcanzar

Al amanecer
Ya no va a llover
Y el pueblo de Pájaro—flor primaveral—
Volverá a nacer

Lluvia hermosa pero aterradora
Podría atacar a cualquier hora
Fue en marzo el 11
Era medianoche
Lluvia con venganza
Hundió calle, casa y coche

La barranca se quebró
El pueblo se inundó
Y el pobre campesino
Sin su casa se quedó

Yo quiero salir, no quiero morir
Qué horror veo pero más dolor tengo
Qué fría el agua ya no hay nada
Apenas tuve chanza de sobrevivir
El dolor como corriente

Llenando los cuartos
Personas huyendo con bolsas en la mano
Saliendo de la casa
Con padres y hermanos
Llevando la tristeza
Llegando con horror y temor pero intacto
Hasta la feria familia

Deja de llorar...

Mojando a todos alrededor del pueblo
Traumados, cansados
Desesperados evacuados
La tristeza nos lleva a donde no sé
Sin iglesia sin escuela pero con alma y fe

Personas heridas
Casas destruídas
Comunidad entera
Rezando por su vida

El 2023 nunca olvidaré
Sin escuela y sin iglesia
Pero con fe y alma seguiré

Con el desastre de ese día
Ten compasión
Por los negocios y puestos
Que sufrieron la inundación

Un río de llanto se desbordó

Pero volver volver
Aunque no sé qué hacer
Pájaro como flor
Lo veré renacer

Deja de llorar...

Yacsiri Zamora, Grade 9
Pájaro Valley High School, Santa Cruz
Sandra Macías, Classroom Teacher
Bob Gómez, Poet-Teacher

Nature's Music

Birdsong is a lighthouse, its beam cutting
through the darkness of silence.
Birdsong is little butterflies, flitting
through the flowers.
It's the ocean waves, each different.
A stream, small but powerful.
Birdsong is like building a nest, each note
is a little stick or a little bit of grass.
Birdsong is a tiger, each tweet, a stripe.
It's the leaves falling from the tree,
swirling in the wind, a knife
cutting through the silence.
Birdsong is like moss climbing slowly
up the tree to reach sunlight.
It's a leopard slinking silently
towards its prey on padded feet.
A waterfall, each note falling to the ground
the way it's supposed to.
Birdsong is like grass springing up after rainfall,
a flower uncurling its petals to create
a rainbow of color.
It's like the mist, its creeping tendrils, notes and tunes.
Birdsong is nature's music.

Samantha Siebert, Grade 4
Edna Maguire School, Marin County
Ann Eshoff, Classroom Teacher
Claire Blotter, Poet-Teachers

There Is A Special Place

Secret of My Soul

My soul is pulling me
taking me to the place
I always go
No one knows
No one can know
Sacred bay of underwater dreams
Dragonflies rest on the
sacred island of secrets,
wings a-glimmering
My soul
is pulling me there
and I come willingly

Finley-Ray Cline, Grade 5
Mattole Elementary School, Humboldt County
Nick Tedesco and Kevin Vesely, Classroom Teachers
Dan Zev Levinson, Poet-Teacher

My Heart

My heart feels like the splashing of Lake Tahoe.
I love taking time, staring into the beautiful water
with fish flowing through the lake's favorite restaurant.
I love going to the pool when it is cold out,
with the crisp air blowing around us,
pushing us to do things we never knew we could.
I love playing ball with my dad in the breezing fast air.
When the ball is in the air, it looks like a crisp leaf
falling from a beautiful, green tree.
I love going on boat sets when we're going fast on the water,
splashing up my face with cool air.
Falling down on our faces feels so good.

James Ghilotti, Grade 4
Prestwood Elementary School, Sonoma County
Katie Grimes, Classroom Teacher
Sandra Anfang, Poet-Teacher

My Special Place

My special place is close, but far
Cold water tickles my toes
The waterfalls look like diamonds
Half Dome shines in the daylight sun
The redwood trees give shade
I smell chicken pot pie filling and biscuits
I can hear water, winding its way here and there
and the sweet sound of birds singing the song of Spring
I see wet morning dew on branches and bushes
I fold up my blankets and puff up my pillow,
change into warm clothes, and walk outside
I play, and I hike, and swim in freezing waters,
enjoying the wonderful, magical, beautiful
    Yosemite

Emily Price-Braschler, Grade 3
Prestwood Elementary School, Sonoma County
Gwen Watson, Classroom Teacher
Sandra Anfang, Poet-Teacher

Watsonville Es

Watsonville es
el pájaro parado en un árbol que canta en las mañanas.
Es el verde de los campos
que se encuentran cercas del pueblo.
Es el pizcador que produce nuestras frutas y verduras.

Watsonville es el pan y chocolate
que los panaderos hacen en las mañanas frías,
es las ardillas que corren por todo el pueblo
sin parar buscando nueces,
es las quinceañeras que hacen cuando las muchachas
cumplen los quince años.

Watsonville es la primavera
llena de color y de alegría de las personas,
es el reggaetón que ponen en los carros para escuchar,
es la admiración de mucha gente
que vive aquí y gente de otros pueblos.

Watsonville es el mural
que describe la agricultura del pueblo y las personas.
Watsonville es el pueblo de la fresa
y de la agricultura de nuestra gente,
y es las familias en la placita
cada viernes con una sonrisa.

Josselyne Contreras-Morales, Grade 9
Pájaro Valley High School, Santa Cruz County
Sandra Macías, Classroom Teacher
Bob Gómez, Poet-Teacher

Before the Snow

Before the snow,
a road hangs
the light of plants
like clean clothes
on a floor

Liam Malik Jayasinha Gray, Grade 5
Fair Oaks School, Los Angeles County
Ericka Irwin, Classroom Teacher
Alice Pero, Poet-Teacher

In The Heart Of Japan

Kimonos flowing
On pretty porcelain skin
By cherry blossoms

In a glossy pond
Beautiful koi fish drifting
In the cool water

The chattering crowd
Is gazing at Mount Fuji
Mist floating below

As the golden moon
Covers the city at night
It is still not quiet

Audrey Sherwood, Grade 4
Lu Sutton Elementary School, Marin County
Pamela Stutzman, Classroom Teacher
Michele Rivers Poet-Teacher

Inside A Jeweled Garden

Inside a jeweled garden
Is an oak tree
Swaying in the wind
Inside that oak tree
Is a Jimson Weed
Inside that Jimson Weed
Is a wet dew drop
I am the white Rose
Growing in the
Moonlit garden
My petals are velvety
Like an old page from a book

Beatrix Foudy, Grade 5
West Portal Elementary School, San Francisco County
Marina DeGroot, Classroom Teacher
Susan Terence, Poet-Teacher

Books Beyond

Wonder in the library
piles of books as tall as mountains
adventures waiting to be discovered
diving in among the pages.

Piles of books as tall as mountains
magic, facts, and more are hidden
diving in among the pages
feeling the urge to fly.

Magic, facts, and more are hidden
I have excitement as I turn a page
feeling the urge to fly
whispers and secrets are dug deep.

I have excitement as I turn a page
adventures waiting to be discovered
whispers and secrets are dug deep
wonder in the library.

Sierra Wallace, Grade 3
Apple Blossom Elementary School, Sonoma County
Carrie Miller, Classroom Teacher
Lisa Shulman, Poet-Teacher

Escape From Reality

When I watch them,
I feel my worries wash away.
When I listen to their voice,
I feel calmness and happiness wash over me.
They always make me laugh, smile, and cry,
whether it be from sadness or happiness.
These people don't know the big impact they've had in my life.
In my moment of darkness, they were some of the people
that stayed.

When I watch these people, I escape reality.
I'm no longer focused on my problems.
I am focused on them, the way they laugh,
or the ridiculous things they're doing.
My mind solemnly focuses on them.
I hide from my reality.
I hide away with people I don't know, yet I trust them!
I am able to escape in a world of happiness.
In a world where I don't have to face
the cruel place we call home.

My body may still be here, but my spirit
is in a place I go when I watch them.
These people bring me to a place of happiness;
a place where I'm not judged for being myself;
a place where there are others like me:
people who also want an escape from reality.

They may be YouTubers, characters, artists, or streamers,
but they are my escape from reality.

Mireya Esquivel, Grade 10
Alliance Cindy & Bill Simon Tech High, Los Angeles County
Anna Benavides, Classroom Teacher
Juan Cardenas, Poet-Teacher

My Special Place

In my bedroom,
there is a special
place. I go there
when I'm frustrated.
The way to
open it
is I have
to snap
my fingers
and a special
door bursts
open.

When you enter,
you are greeted
by some
friendly grizzly
bears.
You are in a forest.
It smells like
fresh grass and
honeycombs.
It tastes like
apples
and there are
some activities:

you can swim
and play

exciting games,
like Tic-tac-toe.
You can eat
anything you want.

Melissa Cabrera, Grade 3
Chenoweth Elementary School, Merced County
Amy Brown, Classroom Teacher
Dawn Trook, Poet-Teacher

Autumnal Forest

The trees shed their brown coat
A leaf flutters to my velvet nose
My soft fluffed ears tilt back in interest
I arch my neck to the dusk light
A gentle crooning leaves my throat
An owl perches on a fungaled log
My tail sweeps the fallen life
I run, quickly and silent
I see people
They grow quiet
I beckon them to follow but,
Only one does,

You

Following to a clearing
With just a simple cream blanket
Watching a lake
Lights strung on a fence
Join me under the apple tree
While the air is still warm
Join me to observe the lake's tide
To watch to stars
Hear the bird turn home
Lay down
Let the blanket comfort you
Breathe the breeze
It will be all right

Let your tears cry
Stay for however long you'd like
Let the Earth calm you.
Rest.

Brianna J. Clayton, Grade 7
Manchester School, Mendocino County
Amy Ruegg, Classroom Teacher
Blake More, Poet-Teacher

Shadow Comes

The tree full of apples
They fall and bruise but never break

When night comes it's like the tide coming
When the sun comes high in the sky, the tides rise

foaming like hair and objects on it
like fences combing hair

Ava Irwin, Grade 6
Fair Oaks School, Los Angeles County
Ericka Irwin, Classroom Teacher
Alice Pero, Poet-Teacher

The Backlit Kitchen In Afterhours

the light bulb in the left corner of the ceiling
needs to be changed.
it keeps flickering every few seconds,
that I doubt the moths are even interested anymore.

there's a rather distasteful stain on the ground
where dish soap meets forgotten produce:
a messy aftermath of a busy shift.

days-old spinach is stuffed in mortar
and the laundry bag decides to tear again
right when I drag it downstairs.

but
when garlic peels floating to the ground
start to look like the seeds of maple trees,
and the churning of the dishwasher
dissolves into a gentle hum,
and the commercials on the radio
fade into bossa nova,
and the broomstick in my hands
looks just a little more like a certain someone,

i understand
that you can't appreciate a day's hard work
without loving the mess it leaves behind.
that you can't wipe a brow in relief
without feeling just how sore your arms are.

that you can't really have any of the extraordinary
without all the ordinary.

because, what do they call it, mundanity?
isn't that word just beautiful?

Ella Wen
Sonoma County Youth Poet Laureate

I Want to Give You

I want to give you a *gabi* of *berde*
mga water lily lumalaki in the *ilog*,
For you a sky of peace in the winter
Here is a dream of pearl violins smiling
Dance with the jade *mga bituin sa dagat*
Laying in the sapphire clouds
Surround yourself with a *langit* of *kapayapaan*
Taste the imagination surrounding you
Hear the inspiring words around you
Embrace the Inspiration that you have heard
I want to give you a night
For you, a sky of peace
Here is a place where you inspire others.

gabi - night
berde - green
mga water lily - water lilies
lumalaki - growing
ilog - river
mga bituin sa dagat - sea stars
langit - sky
kapayapaan - peace

Clareese Regala, Grade 4
Longfellow Elementary School, San Francisco County
Victoria Lanterman, Classroom Teacher
Susan Terence, Poet-Teacher

I Don't Forget My Roots

Sojourner Truth

Picture her leaving behind a life that was not hers
Picture her wounded, pushing through snow and ice
Picture her persisting as hope faded
and the country ventured into war

I like to think of her rising above
the crumbling world,
then building it up again
I like to think of her leaving behind those
who told her to give up

She was the title of her story
A soaring soul above the world
She was a rainbow of jewels
shining in the blackened sky
She was the star that would not blink out

Alexa Riseman, Grade 5
West Portal Elementary School, San Francisco County
Marina DeGroot, Classroom Teacher
Susan Terence, Poet-Teacher

Kazoku

I am the son of Aztec marigolds
and vibrant sugar skulls

The brother of 12 siblings and poverty
The echoes of screaming children
And overfilled apartments in California

I am the cruddy, mundane farms
that are ignored on road-trips
The bitter feeling of being an adult at 10

I'm the bird who fell out of the nest,
the pup that ran away from home,
the one studying the gun in hand,
rather than how to steer a wheel

My soul has come to recognize the shouts of men
mercilessly killed like dogs,
images of the deep, crimson, bloodstained, fields of Korea,
which never fail to lay in the back of my mind

Hiding in humid, lonely trenches
Listening to the distorted music of bullets
Understand the ugly cycle of life and death

The familiar image of lives
blatantly taken from their bodies,
the bloodlust of my flesh-stained bayonet

At any moment, I could be the one painted crimson red
The one on the other side of the gun
The cold body deprived of a soul
Just another dog tag

I come from orange painted skies in Southern California
and endless strawberry fields

I come from understanding my loose grasp
of where I belong, of who I am
Understanding war, death, and love
Understanding that I do have a home
I do have love and family,
but it has yet to find me

Valentine Tileh-kooh, Grade 9
Lowell High School, San Francisco County
Christian Villanueva, Classroom Teacher
Susan Terence, Poet-Teacher

El Corrido de Alicia Rocha

Un 18 de marzo
Santa Cruz era el pueblo
Mi madre Alicia nació
bajo un sol bien dorado

Sus padres son michoacanos
Las amigas la amaban
Pensó en lo que dejaría
Ella siempre trabajaba

Llegó y su vida cambió
Ella vivió con familia
Jugaba con sus hermanas
Antes de darme la vida

Luego encontró su amor
Totalmente ella cambió
Siguió viviendo su vida
Y su nueva vida soy yo

Joshua Montejano, Grade 10
Watsonville High School, Santa Cruz County
Juan Carlos Pozo Block, Classroom Teacher
Bob Gómez, Poet-Teacher

Your Mexican-American Immigrant (Mother)

I come from where the sun gleams like a pearl,
directing its light of yellow rays down onto the green grass.
My hawk eyes watch over the black and white cows
grazing the wet grass, the tan horses with long brown manes
prancing with elegance, and the small, fluffy chickens
clucking with excitement.

While watching over the magnificent horses,
the loud mooing cows, and squawking chickens,
mis manos hold onto the sticky blue *paleta* from the man
with a cream-white ice cream cart.
The *heladero* lights up my life on this small,
quaint home of mine.
Bursts of sugar and bubblegum pieces
scatter throughout my tongue.
Mama calls me over.
My eyes follow, because I know that *cena* is ready.

To understand me, you have to eat *sopa* for dinner.
Sopa is happiness in a bowl of bubbling red tomatoes,
chicken seasoning and alphabet pasta.
Mama pours her love and care into the bowl
with each ladle she scoops.
Her hands are a machine, working and working
until the savory smell fills the entire house.

I grab a yellow ceramic bowl and a silver spoon.
Mama pours in red deliciousness and I look at the *sopa* in awe.

Tomato and salt hit my tongue, like fireworks in the night sky.
Bursts of red tomatoes and chicken seasoning
create a river of flavors, invading
all the crevices in my mouth.
I am ecstatic.

I've known that my affectionate home is a part of who I am
to the jet black birds that fly over,
to the small, pink worms that find their homes in the wet dirt that
grows into the flowers that bloom with grace and divinity.
So, to get my airplane ticket reading San Francisco means leaving
the *heladero* home I've known.

I am the daughter of cow manure and plants
and the daughter of a bustling city.
Yo recuerdo mi vida del sol
where my body would sweat non-stop
and where I took care of the many animals
and walked on the hard gravel to school.
Pero ahora también, yo soy la hija de la niebla
that rolls down the many hills of San Francisco.
I am a combination of loving experiences
and stunning memories.
I am Mexican-American.

Mis manos - My hands
Paleta - Popsicle
Heladero - ice cream man
Cena - dinner
Yo recuerdo mi vida del sol - I remember my life from the sun

Pero ahora también yo soy la hija de la niebla –
    But now I am also the daughter of the mist
Sopa - soup

Jacqueline Ibarra, Grade 9
Lowell High School, San Francisco County
Jacqueline Moses, Classroom Teacher
Susan Terence, Poet-Teacher

My Mom

after If I Told Him: A Completed Portrait of Picasso by Gertrude Stein

Mom and mom mom mom my mom my mom here
my mom there my mom is everywhere.
Mom mom mom mom she mom she she she she
works really hard hard work work really really
there they're here here everywhere.
she mom mom mom she cooks cooks cooks cooks
she cooks the food food food food.
she mom she mom mom mom she is is is happy happy happy.
she laugh laugh laugh when I laugh laugh laugh.
beautiful beautiful mom and mom my mom my mom is here
is here is here is here there there there my mom is everywhere.

Caledonia 'Calla' Palmer, Grade 6
Mill Valley Middle School, Marin County
Coleman Sawyer, Classroom Teacher
Claire Blotter, Poet-Teacher

My Family

My grandma Mary
feeds me the power
of flashbacks and love

My dad who is sick/worried
Every time I hug my dad
his heartbeat is soft and loud

My dad is my kind body
and I am his loud heart

My dad is the soft sea
My mom is the sweet tiger
My grandma is an angel

Every time I see my brother
he is the shooting star
He sets your heart on fire
like a burning star in the sky

My grandma is my angel wings
and I am her eyes
She is my halo
and I am her legs
like the first time I saw the sun

Kojis King Jr., Grade 5
Longfellow Elementary School, San Francisco County
Sheryl Carrillo, Classroom Teacher
Susan Terence, Poet-Teacher

Pondering YuHuang

Gently sloping hills
and large plots of rice farms
seem to go on forever.
One sun where there were once ten.
As the heat beats down on my head, I wonder

How did it feel?
To order the execution of your own
sons - the suns.
To be shot from the sky,
fallen to earth in a blaze of glory
that only brought fear.

How did it feel?
To watch
as your daughter
was stolen from you?
To watch
as she fell in love
with the very same man
who stole her from you?
Did it justify separating her
from her love for all eternity?
Did it justify making that choice for her?

Perhaps He deserved it,
The unending loneliness of losing His children.
Perhaps it was punishment
as he received the authority of an Emperor.

Where there is Yin,
there must be Yang,
and there must always be balance.
Ba taught me that.

Is it wrong, to think
our Heavenly Father is
cruel,
vain,
unfair?
Maybe it is.
And maybe,
just maybe,
it's okay to believe
in something
different,
to have my own
opinion,
interpretation,
belief.

HA.
Her Ma would beat her with a stick if she knew.

She trudges home slowly, her back bent
from the weight of expectations,
clenching the basket of vegetation in her fists.

Watching her silhouette as she walks,
you could almost see
how she'd live the rest of her life:

here,
forever.
Trapped.

Isabella Chan, Grade 9
Lowell High School, San Francisco County
Christian Villanueva, Classroom Teacher
Susan Terence, Poet-Teacher

Maya Angelou

Picture her stories
that you hear.

Picture her poems
and sing them as songs.

Picture her poems
as an inspiring tool.

I like to think of her
as a living poem.

Aria Liu, Grade 5
West Portal Elementary School, San Francisco County
Marina DeGroot, Classroom Teacher
Susan Terence, Poet-Teacher

Life Is Like A Broken-Winged Bird

I am...
My mom's only son.
My kid's beloved father.
My sibling's oldest brother.
My nephew and nieces' uncle.
For a better life for me and my family,
I left my hometown,
traveled over the seas to San Francisco
where I didn't know anyone or understand
any of their languages.
I nervously and excitedly waited for this day to come.

After 3 months...
We landed on the deck,
everyone was provoked to see
the yellow and pale orange sunset.
When I stretched my head out the window,
I felt the harsh wind hitting my brown soft cap.
It felt very dreamy to be in this place,
but this is where my nightmare started.
We were trapped.
Everyone needed a pass to go through the gate to a small boat.
People were scared and confused.
I was too,
but I had to stay calm.

Days passed...
We were questioned many times.

I see the people around me leaving, one by one.

My heart started beating faster and faster.

At that one moment, I felt like I couldn't catch my breath.

Very confused and don't know what to do.

On the cold and windy deck,

I looked at the sea,

hearing the waves rushing up to shore,

looking at the gray and white full moon.

My tears filled the ponds of my eyes.

It hit the top of my heart,

tears start rolling down my cheeks,

like droplets of fog water

rolling down the windows.

" 我真的好想我的家人，我是不是不应该来。 "

I told myself,

" 为了家也要拼了 "

Stared up at the moon and reminded me,

We are looking at the same moon together

from different places.

Months passed...

The white man walked into my room,

He said, *You, You, You, and... You come over here.*

I froze;

I wasn't sure if he pointed at me.

At that moment, I was nervous and anxious.

My roommates and I followed him to the deck.

The bright sun was shining toward my eyes.

I looked across the sea and saw the red and orange
Golden Gate Bridge.

I got on a small, wooden boat going to the railroad company.
A flock of crows landed on the seat right next to mine,
dissecting and eating the dead rat.
This reminds me of my mom telling me
that seeing a crow is bad luck.

我真的好想我的家人，我是不是不应该来 - I miss my
family, was I not supposed to come?

为了家我也要拼了 - For the family, I have to fight this hard war
(not war against someone, a war against his emotions)

Lok Yan Ng, Grade 9
Lowell High School, San Francisco County
Jacqueline Moses, Classroom Teacher
Susan Terence, Poet-Teacher

From the People's Republic to the United States

We were farmers, laborers; the poor of China.
Across the great, vast Pacific was a gleam,
a star of hope, one for a better day, a better life.

I've decided: We're going to live in the United States,
just like my predecessors. It's full of massive, shiny, silver cities,
huge colleges, and job opportunities galore.
We'll make a new life here, instead of the slow, green flatlands of
the Chinese countryside.

We pack our bags and say goodbye to the family and friends we'd
known all our lives, the dusty, winding roads
of sand and gravel, the seemingly endless plains of Guangzhou
filled with farms, the bustling streets of Zhaoqing,
and we go West,
into the land of the unknown,
the land of the rich,
the happy,
the educated.

Everything's been finalized. I hope my daughter
learns English and fits in with her American counterparts.
It'll be fine: the Chinese spirit is within us
and the gods shall accompany us
through our story.

After the long, monotonous plane ride,
red, white, and blue are our new colors.

No longer are we only defined as yellow and red.
I miss the days when I was home - the fun of playing outside
with my cousins, the joy of hanging out with my friends,
and even the dense, humid air in China.

Instead, I was thrust into a land of a different tongue,
one vastly different from mine, and I have no knowledge
of the Western World or its culture.
We migrated from a land with five yellow stars
to a land with fifty white stars.
Our journey was long, and the reward?
Ambiguous.
How much strife?
How much suffering?

The warm, sunny Chinese countryside is being slowly forgotten,
replaced with the urban, industrial American city.
The spring blossoms have long withered, yet we still carry on.
All we can do now is raise this new generation,
to have them mature and grow into something
we can be proud of.

Andrew Chen, Grade 9
Lowell High School, San Francisco County
Jacqueline Moses, Classroom Teacher
Susan Terence, Poet-Teacher

The Final Lesson

I am from a family with fire for hair,
rosy cheeks that are more sunburn than flush,
and eyes like the ocean - glimmering and blue

School is of filthy classrooms with kids packed in like sardines
and teachers that taught me more about adults
than they did about math and writing

I come from kicking rocks down dirt roads
and making dolls from rough sticks and straw
that tickled my fingertips
Real dolls are for the wealthy
is a lesson I learned early from my mum

I am from begging for a meal less mundane than potatoes
or porridge, from stealing lemons off my neighbor's lawn
with my two brothers
They make our faces scrunch and our lips pucker
Lemons are not for eating plain
is a lesson I learned with my brothers flanking my sides

I am from hushed whispers behind closed doors
Ten dinner plates shrink to five
Mum's favorite set of green glass rings goes missing next
and even Dad's dress shoes that he used for special occasions
disappear one day

I force myself to move on from missing objects, because soon
I am from a cramped boat that smells like sweat and laundry that
never thoroughly dried

I learn to keep my head down and eat quickly,
no matter how dry or stale the bread is
Inattention is a good way to be mugged, to go hungry
is a lesson I learn surrounded by starving, greedy people

The once-comforting ocean: blue like Dad's eyes,
calm like Mum's bedtime embrace,
is something I began to detest

When we leave the boat, my legs are jelly
The flames of my hair are tangled and inches shorter
A new city stares back at me
I want to go back to Ireland, I think to myself
The response I get from my despaired prayer
is not what I'd hoped for, but rather the squawking of gulls,
the irritating clickety-clack of heeled shoes on pavement,
and my mother's hand on my back, ushering me forward

Death is real - not just something you hear in stories
or read in Mum's worn-down books
is a lesson I learned in a place far from home

I was not a flower person before
but now, I am from hand-picked dandelions and lillies,
the cleanest weeds I could scavenge,
and poppies vibrant as my brother's hair
tied into a bouquet with waxy string

Me and my brother
(my only brother now)
share a lemon while we weep,
standing before a grave

My tears mix with lemon juice on my tongue
Salty and sour, like the feelings in my heart

Cherish the time spent with your siblings
is the final lesson of my childhood
and a lesson I learned too late

Adeline Kelley, Grade 9
Lowell High School, San Francisco County
Jacqueline Moses, Classroom Teacher
Susan Terence, Poet-Teacher

El Corrido de Tamir Rice

Sucedió allá por Ohio
Vivió un niño sin igual
Tamir Rice era su nombre
Jugaba con juguete en paz

Pero un día llegaron
Los policías al lugar
Confundieron su pistola
Con una real sin dudar

Dispararon sin pensarlo
Y Tamir cayó al suelo
Sólo tenía 12 años
Su vida se fue en un destello

La comunidad se unió
Pedían justicia y verdad
La impunidad se impuso
Y el dolor no pudo sanar

Hoy Tamir es un recuerdo
De lo injusto que es el mundo
Su nombre nunca olvidado
Memoria en cada segundo

Víctor Padilla, Grade 10
Watsonville High School, Santa Cruz County
Juan Carlos Pozo Block, Classroom Teacher
Bob Gómez, Poet-Teacher

Dear Puna,

I come from the broken stories
whispered through bleeding lips,
The threat of war
The deep green shades block everything,
even the flickering light of hope
Blackout

My home is the community in which my ancestors
fought, funded, and found pearls in clams

I come from the whistle of the ocean,
an echo of my own thoughts,
the sand squished between my toes,
our drawings fading, like memories
washed away by the tide

I've always known the ring of the library cart,
devouring every word, traveling the world in my mango tree

I come from the voice of reason soaring,
a songbird over a cross,
the unity of choir,
my sister's hands clasped, hearts so full they burst

My people are ones like me, who have clawed their way
through the burning flames of discrimination
Being the first,
Why must I always lead?

I come from the heavy weight of history,
the boulders of stories
Unshared, It dies with me

I've known the scraping quilts of my Grandmother
and the blanket forts with my cousins
Each square tells a story

I come from the handsewn clothes of my mother
gracing my Christmas tree every year
until they stop

My soul has known that I am strong,
my bones holding up the weight of my world,
never failing
But when my weary bones break,
and the weight of my world will fall,

Dear Puna, you have withstood it all.

Eva Kirschner, Grade 9
Lowell High School, San Francisco County
Christian Villanueva, Classroom Teacher
Susan Terence, Poet-Teacher

Mountainous Walls

*in recognition of Asian immigrants detained
at Angel Island 1910-1940*

Outside I see mountainous walls.
I miss the soft rice fields beneath my feet.
We remember a land of freedom, far beyond this prison.
I feel like I am running in place, getting nowhere,
even if I run myself to death.
Being at Angel Island is like living in a shrinking box,
losing more and more freedom.
We wish to grow wings and fly out to glorious freedom
and prove that they cannot keep us caged.
but alas I know nothing,
I have nothing,
I control nothing,
I am treated like nothing,
but I am not nothing.

Kaya Borovik-Witowski, Grade 5
West Portal Elementary School, San Francisco County
Marina DeGroot, Classroom Teacher
Susan Terence, Poet-Teacher

Still Life of a Strange Yesterday

Where to begin?
Me, the third child of four
Raised under New York's bright lights
We moved with the job
My best memories come
from long summers spent at the farm -
Bloodroot House, only 6 years old,
sleeping in the barn
Christmas in July, raising young cows and pigs
to be slaughtered, like clockwork, in August
no, they don't want you at home
does it seem lonely to you? not as lonely
as the nights when the house shook
with the blows of angry words,
then quieted again
Yes, I had a good childhood
at least, one that shaped me,
taught me to be self-sufficient, independent
taught me to survive
Raised by my sisters, sneaking off to church
just to see what all the fuss is about
Stealing holy water (forgive us)
Perhaps piety could mend the cracks in this dollhouse
And when our family was split in two,
fractured along the coasts,
I was left alone, waiting
I believe she wanted to be a good mother

Wrong place, wrong time, wrong person
She was trapped, wings clipped,
so she tore out feathers until she bled

And my father, he could not face the hurt
a marriage that crumbled like clay
but I will not live with anger, nor regret
Young bride, husband at war
Worked to support our young children
I will make it better for them
I will not repeat the mistakes of those long gone
And yet, I wonder
Perhaps we could have fit together
had there not been madness in our souls
Blood and tears passed on,
twisted heirloom
Bitter is our family legacy.

Maren Brooks, Grade 9
Lowell High School, San Francisco County
Anne Torres, Classroom Teacher
Susan Terence, Poet-Teacher

Colorful Flying Fish

I descended from the pale clouds into the school of brown,
rotting fish. Mr. 徐 hurled me onto the oily conveyor belt to make
leather belts, flattening pieces of rough cattle skin, emitting a
revolting smell. Every salted, egg yolk-colored sundown and
sunrise over and over and over.

The tyrant covered in rainbow badges reigned power over us.
Shipped to the humid, dark green forests of East China.
Given an abundance of arms and speeches emphasizing our
importance, but I sense we are used like lab rats injected with
viruses. Watched as we floundered helplessly.

We moved in squads, just as pawns on a white and black
chessboard, gaining and losing meaningless territory for the
wealthy gold, silver, and black earth we were standing on.
The forest stared at me, absorbing parts of me, unseen,
shaking and warm, eyes wide and traumatized.

Hands were covered in the deep pooling wine red, wrapping
around the wrinkles and old, silver watch given before Mr. 徐
went back into the clouds.

Splattered with cool-infested mud. Wading across
the muddy water, avoiding gunfire and minefields.
Rolls of red dynamite on the bridge, fuse lit.

Pressure sends us flying, enough to outfly an eagle
diving for a defenseless white mouse.

Leaving the bridge and train tracks in the past,
along with my unsettling consciousness.

I live in a two-floor apartment shared with twenty-five;
Amongst were children, my wife, my father, and me.
Red tags on every door, to scare dark demons away.
Feeding the dancing lion cabbages around the smoking and
crackling firecrackers, emitting and leaving behind burnt red
paper scraps, now soaking in the rain destined to be
paper mâché. My taped flip-flops and patched clothes
drag across the pouring rain.
Patter, Patter, Patter
The rain isolates all noises.
The singing of 鄧麗筠
playing on the deserted radio,
but all I had left remains
at that very bridge

徐 – Xu, Chinese Surname
鄧麗筠 - Teng Li-Yun, popular singer from the 1930s

Raphael Xu, Grade 9
Lowell High School, San Francisco County
Jacqueline Moses, Classroom Teacher
Susan Terence, Poet-Teacher

Cans

leave the broken land.
leave the broken jungle.

leave quickly; don't look back.
leave everything; don't look back.

Việt Nam cannot live again.
Won't rebirth like a
Phượng Hoàng.

leave on a dinky boat
for the fisher.

for land many xích,
where the crow flies.

the fish of what the fishermen fished.
fish in a can.
can of food and food.

a can for your troubles?
2 cans for your troubles?

can the cans can the troubles?
can the cans expel the fear?
can the cans return the wealth?
can the cans replicate the old?

all the present?
all the past?
all the future?

left quickly; did not look back.
left everything; did not look back.

can a can be the future?
can a can help our young?
can cans bring us away?

land of the cans
can create a new home.
land of the cans
can build an American dream.

Nicholas Sin, Grade 9
Lowell High School, San Francisco County
Allison Kent, Classroom Teacher
Susan Terence, Poet-Teacher

Amanda Gorman

Picture her writing at the speed of light
Picture her saying
a poem from a crystal ball

I like to think of her
writing what she wants
not what others want

I like to think of her
reading a speech to the world

Julia Torre, Grade 5
West Portal Elementary School, San Francisco County
Marina DeGroot, Classroom Teacher
Susan Terence, Poet-Teacher

Free

i have landed in the land of the free,
yet i feel not any more freedom, in fact,
i feel suppressed by unfamiliar alphabetic words
i come from ideographic symbols
elegant, flexible, monosyllabic structures
i come from giving the last piece of meat
to my younger siblings
no tasty treats
overwatered congee, just to get by
but here in the land of the free,
small chinese pastry shops offer me
juicy pork buns, pineapple buns, steamed buns
stomach grumbles
my fingers wander over the infinite choices
gazing at goods i could not afford

i am the son of living in the rural mountains
        walking miles down to broken-down city streets
        only to barely make a dollar a day
i am the son of meals with sparse scraps of food
        savoring every last grain of rice
        skipping meals when there is not enough
despite being new here, in the land of the free
i study these alphabetic words until
they are no longer unfamiliar
i am both a waiter and a mailman

whether it's light out or obsidian dark outside
whether i am hit by falling raindrops or sweating,
hotter than 100.4° F
i persevere
to bring mouth-watering foods to every meal
dark under eyes, but
i am determined
the stories of *wu ya he shui*
    the "make the impossible, possible" mindset
my descendants will be the sons and daughters of
    living in the bustling city, much opportunity
    long history of medical professions
my descendants will be the sons and daughters of
    eating until they are about to burst
    breakfast, brunch, lunch, supper, dessert

now, i pass by that chinese pastry shop
and once again,
my nose is tickled by the honey-sweet scent of fresh baked buns
except this time, i am sitting
brushing over my lips with a white cloth
crumbs
i am no longer suppressed
by unfamiliarity,
poverty,
instead,
i am
free

Emily Lau, Grade 9
Lowell High School, San Francisco County
Jacqueline Moses, Classroom Teacher
Susan Terence, Poet-Teacher

From the Little Village of Masefau (Grandma)

I come from the little village of Masefau,
where the trees stretch like clouds
and the way the ocean is your neighbor.

My bare feet soaking in the rich, brown dirt
causing my feet to stain.
The *Gardenias* dance with the wind
as it blows to the waves of the ocean.
The curls of my hair bouncing each time I take a step.

I watch from a distance:
My mom dances with the ocean, letting it guide her light.
I watch from a distance:
My land, My family, My people.

The sounds of the chickens singing together
are the things to wake up to.
The sounds of the little ones playing around
and drawing in the sand with sticks, like pencil to paper.
The men cooking the meat over the raw fire,
while the fire spreads as much as it can.
The delicious, savory smell made my stomach turn,
leap, and jump through the air.

The scenery of the mountains standing so tall,
caving us in and protecting us.
The touch of one gardenia can do so much,
even though it's so little.

With grace, plucking the flower off the green stem
that is holding its heart,
holding the flower in my hand, like it's a baby.
I tuck the flower behind my right ear
and hum to the sound of the ocean, closing my eyes shut.
I breathe the air, letting it sink through
and cracking my eyes back open.
The almonds in my eyes watching everyone.

The land of Masefau has so many colors,
even though it's built out of one rainbow.

I turn from a distance to watch my kids be kids.
I love my family; they bring me joy, like when kids have candy.
I want them to feel comfortable in Masefau,
where they can grow like flowers.

I feel a tug at the end of my wrap on my leg.
La'u pepe, Suliana.

My youngest, her eyes so big, like the sun shining through.
We both turn our heads to watch the sunset go down.
I turn to look back at Suliana.
She is the pink flower that sticks out,
bright in the white flower garden.
Oi la'u pepe teine, Suliana.

I want to stay, just stay at my home.
Lo'u fale, Masefau.
I want my little ones to grow so much and be so much more.
I want the moon to take me and drive me away,

to guide my kids to each star.
Lo'u fale, Masefau.

Gardenias - flowers
La'u pepe - My baby
Oi la'u pepe teine - Oh, my baby girl
Lo'u fale, Masefau - My home, Masefau

Dalayah Feiloakitau-Johnson, Grade 9
Lowell High School, San Francisco County
Anne Torres, Classroom Teacher
Susan Terence, Poet-Teacher

Roots

Go, she says
quietly, softly, *you need to go.*
The plane entrance gapes at me, a maw of uncertainty,
a portal into this place called America,
where bananas are more than five inches long?!
and disagreeing won't get you disappeared.
I have known isolation and guarded silence,
the bitter shields of continuous fear:
Don't make friends, don't go anywhere, keep your eyes down.
I am the daughter of steamed rice and inkbrush calligraphy,
	bold strokes of black ink,
writing exam answers for dear life, for a life away. from. here.
a life in America.
	White puffs of breath
	blowing steam from rice with sesame oil and soy sauce
on the snow-frosted walk to school.
My soul holds close
laughter-tossed
dusk-painted
guavas
tugged from neighbors' trees.
Crepes with sesame and molasses, skillet-seared
until it's thin as the paper from Baba's factory.
Sweet nectar fragrance screened by acrid, coal stove smoke.
They warned me about the gnarly bureaucracy:
they did not warn me enough.

At home, my life hung by a single, flimsy, aluminum staple,

holding a packet of forms together
as a banker casually flings it onto a towering pile
of similar forms.
As I watch the enormous heap of paper on the bank counter,
as I pray that the staple will hold,
that my life will not scatter like leaves before a monsoon storm,
at least there was only one packet of forms.
Here, there are tendrils of forms and paperwork
going in infinite circles,
a canopy of obstacles
in this land of haves and have-nots.
Brutal exams mean
burning eyes instead of midnight oil
as I hold down the thrashing dragon of a job and a degree.

What if I don't make it here?
What if I run out of money?
What if the law fails me, like so many others?
I fight. I smile. And I don't forget my roots.

Akhilandeshwari Krishnan, Grade 9
Lowell High School, San Francisco County
Anne Torres, Classroom Teacher
Susan Terence, Poet-Teacher

The Tendrils Of My Mind

I Can't Write A Poem

Forget it. You must be joking.
I have no clue what to write.
It takes too much time to do this.
There's no way I can do this.
It's much too complicated.
My brain is aching just from thinking.
It's too hard to write such a hard form of writing.
Can I do this another day?
Times up. Oh no – what do I do?
All I have is a lot of excuses
(I mean, good reasons).
You think it's good?
Stop joking.
I appreciate it.
Should I make another one?

Tlaloc Pacheco, Grade 6
Willowside Middle School, Sonoma County
Nicola Niedermair, Classroom Teacher
Brennan DeFrisco, Poet-Teacher

The Violin Miracle

I live in the world of music
Where no other thing matters
Except the endless singing
Of the brown, boneless body
Seemingly plain, but full of joy and heart
Sleek, shining bright
He plays into the night
And yet, the bow keeps on bowing
And the strings keep on moaning

If the hollow, maple body
Were to pause its song,
The strings would play
That very day,
A very melancholy song
The paint makes it beautiful
The rosin has the bow
make the strings play a
Pretty sound

The G string makes it low
The E string's really high,
As if it were on fire,
But D is in the middle,
Like a little liar
A is almost high as E,
But it gives you less of a scare
All give a pretty sound,

As pretty as the sky
So always appreciate the violin,
and in the air, you'll fly!!!!

Oceanna Stewart, Grade 5
Strawberry Point School, Marin County
Daniel Gasparini, Classroom Teacher
Terri Glass, Poet-Teacher

The Moon

I want to go to the moon
but I need to make a rocket ship
so I make a rocket ship
and I need to
make it out of UFOs
then, I took off
to the moon
but I didn't make it
then, I used
my only can of root beer
to make it the rest
of the way.

Jack Johnson, Grade 3
Chenoweth Elementary School, Merced County
Amy Brown, Classroom Teacher
Dawn Trook, Poet-Teacher

Moon Trip

My moon trip starts
Now.
First,
I had a chair
Then I took
One billion
Sodas and shook
Them up.
I tied them
To the chair
And I lifted off
I landed
2 planets away
The first planet
Was made of candy
I ate enough
I could jump to
The moon, so I did
Before I
could get to the top,
A BFG appeared
And took me home.

A'sante Valentine, Grade 3
Chenoweth Elementary School, Merced County
Amy Brown, Classroom Teacher
Dawn Trook, Poet-Teacher

Lost

Man watching the north star
Finding his way home
He made it, safe and sound

Brilynn Scaramella, Grade 6
Manchester School, Mendocino County
Amy Ruegg, Classroom Teacher
Blake More, Poet-Teacher

Her Name Is Lane

Her mother, Laura.
Her father, Ben.
Her name is Lane,
because she always stays in hers.
All the space she's ever occupied,
year after year.
She dreams her days away
since the wool was pulled over her heart.
She finds trusting others is a game of chance.
She's never been a gambler
because she stays in her Lane.
Her love rides the highway
so, no one can catch her.
Headlights streak
across the eyes of neglected men
like industrial shooting stars.

Vivian Barajas, Grade 12
South Valley High School, Mendocino County
Kita Grinberg, Classroom Teacher
Jabez W. Churchill, Poet-Teacher

Unseen

A staircase to the sky; it goes to nowhere
A piano playing music by itself
Two masks, happy and sad
A vine curling in and out of fence links
The music notes floating away from the piano
A rose with thorns, sharp and prickly
A butterfly dancing

Ashley Watts, Grade 8
Fair Oaks School, Los Angeles County
Ericka Irwin, Classroom Teacher
Alice Pero, Poet-Teacher

My Heart Is Known and Unknown

In my heart is a void, searching the right answers in life
as I cut through the world, like a scythe.

My heart sounds like rain, as I find out
how to deal with pain.

My heart is wondering, Is it God I'm looking for?
or some other European folklore?

My heart is wondering, Do aliens exist?
Is this real or just for appeal?

Is this from my heart or is it from my brain?
Am I smart or practically insane?

Noah Wild, Grade 5
Trillium Charter School, Humboldt County
Katie Dens, Classroom Teacher
Dan Zev Levinson, Poet-Teacher

Confusion

Confusion is a lost child,
Wandering around a maze,
Not knowing how they got there.
They wear a gray and blue striped shirt
And shorts covered with dirt,
Trying to find a way home.

Jillian Gonzalez, Grade 5
Apple Blossom Elementary School, Sonoma County
Carrie Miller, Classroom Teacher
Lisa Shulman, Poet-Teacher

Jealousy

Jealousy wears a dark, ripped coat
with mismatched buttons.

Her long, voluminous hair drags on her back,
tucked behind her ears as she watches everyone
enjoying themselves and having the time of their lives.

Hearing their laughter makes her emotion grow stronger.
Her bitterness causes the sky to rumble with anger.
Jealousy kicks and stumbles over rocks
as she walks away, feeling pity and lonely.

The sound of gloomy, dark, gray records start playing
throughout the dark mountains, as she watches people
laugh and dance from a distance
with only one thought in her head,

Why isn't that me?

Amelia Vela, Grade 6
Mountain View Elementary School, Santa Barbara County
Karis Joldersma, Classroom Teacher
Cie Gumucio, Poet-Teacher

Good Rhymes For Bad Times

Sad?
Alone?
Ashamed?
We don't know.
Dear old time,
Should this poem even rhyme?

Sometimes, it feels like a crime to the mind
to finally be something more than fine.
Love isn't seen in one's disillusioned mind,
far beyond what is visible to the human eye.

Why are you all still here, living in pure fear?
It makes others believe there is a need to shed a tear.

It can be harsh to someone who isn't okay men- tally,
to observe and define everything they see,
so they can eventually evolve and become
something they never desired to be.

We're just kids feeding off of vulnerability,
constantly trying to avoid the thought of
whatever the future might set free
when you stay up wondering what you want to be,
eventually forgetting the definition of 'me.'

We're constantly questioning every horribly, unstable situation
that has simply no backstory in the grand scheme of things
for us, as human beings.

Steps were taken, but steps back had always been preferred.
The lack of wanting to see the sun in the morn- ing,
and being reminded of a day that doesn't want to be started,
corrupts the very point of being called a nerd.
There might be too much time to question who you are
throughout every year of your life, but at least we can let out
our overwhelming in- securities to ourselves,
even if it just consists of yelling at a wall or crying in your bed.

Across every possible intensity of time,
only you can imagine the one you look forward to
while dreaming in your head.
We shall pursue our personal goals and free
the pessimistic mentality we once perceived to be true,
trust others when we say,
eventually you shall understand the missing clue,
even if it rains and the sky is no longer blue.
Nobody should ever enforce you to change, rather than
impact you with something intentionally to give you comfort and
the ability to say it's okay to be strange.
I am sure there is plenty of space to rearrange.
Go ahead and enjoy that long awaited mental climb,
while we forever question whether it is bedtime.

Kimberly 'Kim-bo' Viera, Grade 10
Alliance Cindy & Bill Simon Tech High, Los Angeles County
Anna Benavides, Classroom Teacher
Juan Cardenas, Poet-Teacher

Falafel and Pita

Falafel and pita
  Pita Bread is my future corgi
    The corgi jumped down the stairs
      101 flights of stairs to climb
        Mt. Everest is a trip to climb up
          Up goes the blimp
            Aircrafts fly all the time
              The clock is ticking
            Out of patience little one
          One person left
        Right is wrong
      You can always make mistakes, killer whale
    Baleen whales have thousands of very thin teeth
  One thousand wishes
Genes aren't as good as you think they are
Ideas come naturally
Nature is life
  Living isn't always the best for people
    Eventually the sun will explode, starting the rebirth
      of the Milky Way and will lead
        to the recreation of the universe
          Do parallel universes exist?
          Does time exist or is time
        just in our heads?
      What is consciousness?
    What came first, the colour orange
  or the fruit?

Jenevieve Shaw, Grade 6
Willowside Middle School, Sonoma County
Nicola Niedermair, Classroom Teacher
Brennan DeFrisco, Poet-Teacher

Vividly Colors

Orange is when I peel an orange. It spurts and pops
and stings my fingers. It burns my
eyes. O no, I don't like orange.

Green—don't even get me started
with that. It's the color of vegetables.
It tastes like a possum that got squashed
by a pig and dropkicked into a dumpster.

O, and there's red. Red kind of
scares me, like a clown at night with
a red balloon. Then it pops—shivers go
down my spine. O no, not red.

And white is the color of a page,
like I'm writing an 83-page essay
and it's due tomorrow.

Ellie Harmon, Grade 5
Trinidad Elementary School, Humboldt County
Emmet Bowman, Classroom Teacher
Dan Zev Levinson, Poet-Teacher

Green

I walk out of my house
and see the wet grass.
I go into the green
room in the White House.
My friend's brother has
a green dinosaur that he plays with.
I climb the green hill.
I see all the green trees
when I ride past the street.
I see green on me.

Andrea Orozco, Grade 3
Chenoweth Elementary School, Merced County
Meuy Saeteurn, Classroom Teacher
Dawn Trook, Poet-Teacher

Purple

The heart of every color. The heart of love.
A magical mushroom.
The gathering of all Color.
Purple born from all of them.
Clothes, made of

F
A
I
R
Y

D
U
S
T

and kindness
The raindrop she rides, a beautiful mixture of blues.

T
S
U
Made from seafoam and D
At dusk in the summer,
You can catch a glance.

Katrine Willey, Grade 4
Montecito Union School, Santa Barbara County
Shannon Gallup, Classroom Teacher
Cie Gumucio, Poet-Teacher

Blue Sadness

Sadness, blue as tears.
Sadness feels lonely
like losing a friend.
Sadness feels alone
like when you're by yourself.
Sadness sounds like not being able
to use your cellphone,
like rain trickling in the forest.
Sadness tastes like
swallowing ugly tears,
then, not having dessert.

Sophia Lopez, Grade 4
Logan Memorial Educational Campus, San Diego County
Lindsay Theel, Classroom Teacher
Johnnierenee Nia Nelson, Poet-Teacher

Parents In My Heart

Dad brings love
Dad brings hugs
Dad brings clothes
Dad brings puppies
Dad brings happiness

while mother sends one letter.

Bella Ramos, Grade 4
Logan Memorial Educational Campus, San Diego County
Nate Herron, Classroom Teacher
Johnnierenee Nia Nelson, Poet-Teacher

Melting the Snow

Happiness is like the sun
melting the snow.

Sadness is like the rain,
making everyone feel bad
to break their feelings.

Don't give up.

Jack Gorman, Kindergarten
Alexander Valley School, Sonoma County
Julie Axell, Classroom Teacher
Maureen Hurley, Poet-Teacher

Among the Trees

The tendrils of my mind have found my heart
And spun around it 'till its scars have bled
For every waking thought my soul imparts
Sends dreams of love and laughter to my head
In recent nights, my rest, severed, has stemmed
From visions of a life I can't attain
Yet still, I crave her presence and to mend
My sorrow with her love and perfect brain
Her eyes glow green with mystique forest fire
And set ablaze my being's deepest woods
For in those woods, there lies my deep desire
My memories of Eve, the greatest good
To crucify my heart and set it free
I must confess and heal among the trees

Jackson Bramlette, Grade 12
Redwood High School, Marin County
Kristin Klempnauer, Classroom Teacher
Maxine Flasher-Düzgüneş, Poet-Teacher

Stand

No reason to keep standing up.
Like a sinkhole, falling in the karst land.
Keep running. All the reasons to stop.
Yet why? There are no reasons to stop, thereof.
Nothing to hold onto. Still falling.
No reason to try to stop.
The thrill and adrenaline, coursing through my veins.
I know there will be pain.
Only a split second of it.
Then, everything will go dark.
Everything opaque for miles.
Millenniums passing, nothing changing,
But I have too much adrenaline to feel.
Then, I feel the terrain below.
No pain, No splat.
My excitement dissipating, yet everything is dark.
The ground gives way in a loud rumble and crack.
An arctic chill and a blue like none other.
Clarifying the glacier crevasse.
Massifs of glaciers, all across the land.
Back in the stone age.
Nothing makes sense.
That is my reason to stand.

Enzo Lasek, Grade 6
Willowside Middle School, Sonoma County
Nicola Niedermair, Classroom Teacher
Brennan DeFrisco, Poet-Teacher

The Awesome Adventures of Kane

Kane is in the Dino excavation site with his dad
when he finds an Amethyst in an extravagant Geode
in the hard Sand. He gets so excited that
he bakes an Apple pie!

Kane Minor, Grade 3
Chenoweth Elementary School, Merced County
Meuy Saeteurn, Classroom Teacher
Dawn Trook, Poet-Teacher

Silly Bs

Bulbasaur barfed on the
book about blobfish,
but Blastoise blasted Bulbasaur
and he got blubber to slap
Bulbasaur, but then
Brother Benjamin came and super smash struck
Blastoise with a bronze brick.
Meanwhile, a bee booked a store to blend blond boys,
but a brilliant boy took the bee to a beach by a bay,
the bee told the boy she loved bears, so
the boy dyed his hair brown as a bear
and then told the bee how he also loved bears
and because of that, the bee went to the nearby bay
and got the boy a teddy bear.
But then, a vicious, mischievous, and bald bear attacked.
The boy wanted to protect the bee, so he bravened up
and fought the bear.
Before he knew it, he had won.

Jose Valero, Grade 3
Chenoweth Elementary School, Merced County
Amy Brown, Classroom Teacher
Dawn Trook, Poet-Teacher

Dear Miners,

Walking through the mineshaft,
your hands still shaking from the ride down,
mimicking the shaking of the Manskip
we came down on.
A small ambient glow,
flickering around your head,
just slightly brighter than a firefly.

Black all around,
like a moonless,
cloudy night.
The gold,
like veins of stars in a hollow sky,
more radiant than the sun itself.

The golden lines shine
like their own galaxy.
Swirling and reaching
with ethereal arms,
shining with the light
of a hundred dying stars.

Ella Ely-Lock, Grade 11
Sierra Academy of Expeditionary Learning, Nevada County
Marika Beck, Classroom Teacher
Kirsten Casey, Poet-Teacher

I Wish To Compile

I think it's incredibly fun, being able to sit and learn about the history of the fae and, right after, learn about how humans evolve from a scientific standpoint. I think it's fun to hear about theories on the human mind: its ability to shift its consciousness from one to another, and then hear some hermit's story about how it's impossible wishwash.

I think it's fun to hear both sides of every story and to compile that knowledge together, and just...hold it. Share it.
Let all those little, special people peer into the abilities of the human mind and the stories of our world.
Let all of them fly off, like dandelions, to plant their own roots and overpower those who think that learning and attempting to share all this varied information shouldn't be a thing.

I want to compile all these things just to know.
Just know for the sake of knowing, because there's no need for me to, but I have the most primal need to.
I want to share with the world what it shares with me.
I want to venture into its most hidden caverns
and reach into its deepest oceans
and pull back the brightest, shining treasures from them all
with no reason behind it other than just knowing that it's there.

Other than just learning from it,
it's fun,
it's freeing,
it's what I want to do

and it's what I WILL do.
There is NO ONE out there who can prevent me.
You can't tack down the fragile wings of a butterfly
because no matter where you tack it, it will rip its wings
to leave once more, no matter the risk.

You have to suffice with knowing you will never catch it
to study, because once you do catch it, it would rather die
than let itself be studied alive.
Even under the false presumption that perhaps,
just MAYBE, you could fake it out, you never will.

I want to compile the information of the world,
that of the universe,
that of the entire multiverse
and all its possibilities and plausibilities.
I want to share it.
I want to be the person I once spoke of,
sharing all their secrets of the world with me.
I wish to take her up on her offer
on becoming the next holder of her title.
I want to share once more with the world
what it shared with me.

Aylani 'Nix' Smith Sosa, Grade 10
Alliance Cindy & Bill Simon Tech High, Los Angeles County
Anna Benavides, Classroom Teacher
Juan Cardenas, Poet-Teacher

A Recipe For Ska

Plug in.

Set instruments at max.

Breath in. Notice:

One misty afternoon.

1 director,

1-2 oz of singing,

1 pound of Guitar ,

1 kilogram of Bass,

1 cup of drums,

And a little bit of piano on top.

And play, A beginning guitar solo

Bass comes in, then drums, then singing.

Sweat drips off, as people watch you play, play better
and better

A skateboard ramp on the left of the stage

and graffiti all over the walls, The Phoenix.

A person to sign you in and check your tickets at the
entrance. Perfect—

The other band is getting ready.

About ten more minutes until it's over.

It felt like it happened yesterday

and it's about to happen again!

Johnathan McCloud, Grade 6
Willowside Middle School, Sonoma County
Nicola Niedermair, Classroom Teacher
Brennan DeFrisco, Poet-Teacher

A Recipe for YouTube

Grab millions of creators,
each with self-dignity at the minimum.
One endless world of the internet
Web pages, all weaving together
Countless mountains of content
Hours of watch time
A billion videos

5 hours, maybe more
60 million computers at full volume
7 of the most naive ideas getting billions of views.
Helpless souls getting sucked in,
losing themselves along the way
Sense of self going down the drain

No end in sight—
Eyes burning, hands cramping
Empty containers scattered around
But still, an urge for more
3 distant calls from the other room, easy to ignore
Telling myself to get up, but my legs unable to respond
Finally forcing a surrender,
knowing tomorrow is a new day.

Jack Battuello, Grade 6
Willowside Middle School, Sonoma County
Nicola Niedermair, Classroom Teacher
Brennan DeFrisco, Poet-Teacher

Recipe For A Blizzard

First, melt 56 ice cubes
Stir in a bottle of rain clouds
and add a pinch of tornado powder
Then, add in a tablespoon of hailstones
Finally, sprinkle in 2 cups of snowflakes
Serve on a cold plate in the South Pole.

Jack Matoza, Grade 4
Mountain View Elementary School, Santa Barbara County
Carly Schmiess, Classroom Teacher
Cie Gumucio, Poet-Teacher

Tricky Mickey

A little boy named Mickey
did not like his sister Vicki,
nor his brother Nickey.

Then Mickey became a sickie,
and said, *This is a little tricky,*
in and out of the door, quickie!

Joe Engles, Grade 6
Willowside Middle School, Sonoma County
Cari Cardle, Classroom Teacher
Brennan DeFrisco, Poet-Teacher

Creativity

That piece of paper,
the one who lives on your desk,
the wilderness of creativity—
Possibility lives there.
Be the explorer to discover it.
You slice your pencil on it,
like you're slicing plants.
Cross over other lines, like crossing a lost bridge.

Then,
You finally found it.
You found the lost city of Creativity
Exposed to the world,
the wild creativity will always stay
on that one piece of paper

Valeria Hernandez, Grade 6
Willowside Middle School, Sonoma County
Nicola Niedermair, Classroom Teacher
Brennan DeFrisco, Poet-Teacher

Publishing

publishing is like getting a new pair of socks
it tastes like a birthday ice cream
cake publishing is just like traveling to Hawaii
publishing smells like a tiger
lily publishing is like getting
a new tuxedo or dress but
sometimes it's like a kick in
the head when you don't get
published publishing looks just
like American poppies
publishing is just like getting
a star on your homework
publishing is just like reading an interesting poem
publishing looks like a rainbow
it sometimes sparks into a
flame it also can look like the rising
sun with splashes of pink and blue
i believe it feels like when
you just turn twelve

Rosy Faust, Grade 5
Arcata Elementary School, Humboldt County
Julia Adams, Classroom Teacher
Dan Zev Levinson, Poet-Teacher

This Is For You

I want to give you a night of sapphire blue birds,
soaring in the stars
For you, an ocean of happiness
in the summer
Here is a forest of jade harps,
singing in the fall
Dance with the topaz bobcat,
prancing on the ruby mountain
Surround yourself with a river
of pearl water lilies
Taste the sweetness of the melons
Hear the loud caw of the song sparrows
Embrace the joy and sadness of the world

Rigi Dare, Grade 3
Francis Scott Key Elementary School, San Francisco County
Bonnie Quinn, Classroom Teacher
Susan Terence, Poet-Teacher

I'll Always Believe

I believe in poetry. It feels so right.
It sounds so sweet. I believe that poetry
is a good way to let go of emotions,
so they don't bottle up and blow. When I
write poetry, I feel like I'm in a titanium
box and nothing can reach me. It sounds
like a waterfall in spring. I believe.

Vivian Sweaney, Grade 4
Ambrosini Elementary School, Humboldt County
Alissa Stone, Classroom Teacher
Dan Zev Levinson, Poet-Teacher

Tell The Story To The Wind
Poet-Teacher Poems

Dear Paintbrush,

We are becoming too familiar, it seems
the blue never washes from your sable fibers.
There is too much paint, if you ask me,
this is not a patisserie, and yet it seems you work
with frosting in layers. Your handle is cracking,
a thin piece of wood, whittled from a pine tree
in Normandy. You are worn down, like the pale painter
who stays too long in the garden, his jacket dusted
with yellow pollen. He moves too quickly, is startled
by unoiled hinges and sudden wind through the shutters.
There is paint between his teeth, and his fingernails
are stained. He rarely sets you down, rarely sleeps, rarely
turns from the window, where on the sill, he arranges
the turpentine bottles filled with water—now a row of vases
for bunches of flat-faced sunflowers, as yellow
as the moon glow, the stellar halos, the lamplight
in village windows. I am tightening from the weight of paint.
Once, I was pulled across a wooden frame, but this
is a new burden. Hide yourself, roll under
the rags so he might rest. Let him lie down
in the dark, if only the stars would
go out.

With concern,
The canvas

Kirsten Casey
Poet-Teacher, Nevada County

Helpers

My father always shut the light out for us,
gently removed our glasses, book, pencil
or paper gripped in our hands if we'd dozed off
while intending to read or write.

He brought my mother coffee in the morning,
made his two culinary achievements—toast
buttered on both sides and fein cochen, moist
scrambled eggs.

He was the one who'd wanted the broken down
adobe house in the middle of a barren desert acre.
A sometime city-boy in Chicago or smaller Peoria,
he'd envisioned the West booming with fowl
and livestock, a to-be cowboy's ranch dream.

My mother was no fan of the miniscule house—no dining
room or pantry—but relished the acre's potential for
home agriculture which flourished under her hands—
sweet grapes, crisp asparagus, tart strawberries, melons
like huge dirigibles floating over the dirt.

Later they traded eggs from their hens and ducks for
aromatic rye breads, pumpernickel, and challah from
Eagle Bakery across town.

We were trained by both parents to inherently sense
who needed help, a door open, a kind word, a bowl of soup,
a seedling, a joke, a doll, a jacket, a ride or friend.

We were scouts for others in danger—unwitting captains of small boats on an unruly sea.

My mother once told my brother's daughter, "Remember, we have never been rich or tried to be, but we have always been helpers. Remember that."

Who is not to deny the richness & bounty in sharing—
rather than hoarding an ocean or field for oneself
when really it is there for all to swim in or grow?

Susan Terence
Poet-Teacher, San Francisco County

Pine

our backyard Ponderosa pine (back then we just called it pine tree,
we didn't have pine tree eyes yet)
    I was not scared as long as I fixed on the sky, the
    ground—even soft with dark soil & pine needles—
made me dizzy

if I wasn't in a tree, on a roof, in the air–
    I was always in the sky—blue, smog, rain, the threat of
    rain, the invitation of rain, stars, no stars,
lightning bolts I'd drive towards

my body could be anywhere, in a car, classroom, under you,
dancing to don't you forget about me,
    and I'd be hopping cloud to cloud, a giant hopscotch,
    floating not falling

our backyard pine tree I climbed up & up & off

    there is no earth there is no earth

Dawn Trook
Poet-Teacher, Merced County

Almost

Drop of water
on the edge of the leaf
almost falling

Stars appear
in the nursery rhyme
Child twinkles in and out

The shadow moving with her
has no idea
how it was formed

Stored in a cool, dry place
unmoving mind

Asleep, dreaming of lightning
Awake she cannot hear
distant thunder

Her thought
suspended in ineffable disbelief
arrives where you are

Alice Pero
Poet-Teacher, Los Angeles County

Ukraine

Mostly I walk across the meadow in early morning light,
catching sight of dragon flies flitting above tall grasses as I
listen to the stollen melodies of the mockingbirds.
Sometimes I drift to the shore where gulls and waves are my
companions.
I stand silently, looking at the vastness of the ocean—
Imagination floating across the miles to distant shores.
This is such a stunningly beautiful world.
Yet like millions of others, I bear the dense, black suffering of
the Ukraine with me—wherever my rambling soul wanders.
I want to slip into a rudderless boat,
to carry me away from the harsh reality of life on this earth.
There will be no cargo of loathing, no hate, or the outrageous
cruelty of humanity.
My boat will be full of hope and love—
Carrying heaps of bright yellow sunflowers—
Turning their heads toward the sun.

Michele Rivers
Poet-Teacher, Marin County

In My Lap

peace, contentment,
blessed bliss,
brimming over happiness –
where can it be found?

bakers boast of bread well risen,
builders pride in fine precision,
singers croon melodic notes,
scholars revel in famous quotes,
pigs rejoice in muddy pens,
lazy bears in cozy dens,
resting lions love their lairs,
penguins trust their life long pairs,
bookworms relish reading books,
writers crave their writing nooks,
hikers sigh on wooded paths,
kids relax in bubble baths,

peace, contentment,
blessed bliss,
brimming over happiness –
where can it be found?
only kitten needs no map,
he finds nirvana
in my lap

Michele Krueger
Poet-Teacher, Lake County

Making Community

I wave at them all. Indiscriminately. The mailman.
Middle school girls clutching their phones. Garbage collectors.
A grey-haired woman with a yippy dog. Amazon drivers hustling
between houses. I'm staking. My claim to community. Masked.
Walking alone. Here. Where I can. Past lawns with rainbow
spinning pinwheels. Ceramic owls. Plastic hummingbirds on
sticks. In this strange land. Where I find. My self. The planet.
I never imagined. At home. Grateful. For three redwood trees
towering over my house. Wrapping me in. A kind of peace.
Larger than heavy white monster trucks. Rumbling by.
Revving up. I wave. Smile.

Hello. Neighbor.

Claire Blotter
Poet-Teacher, Marin County

♡ - - - - ♡

San Francisco didn't used to be a love song
wintry & pomegranate stained
the skyline was only for commuters
and the lonely people passing thru for a day
swamped in the boho hymns of their volvo
and the collapsible edges
of their heart
'la vita è bella solo para te'
when going home is like waking up
from the muted vinyl stereo
and your voice steaming up the windshield
my fingers drawing a heart-shape
on the driver's side
and you finally pressing the defroster
like nothing ever happened

Maxine Flasher-Duzgunes
Poet Teacher, Marin County

These Poems

shoutout to June Jordan

These poems are the baby teeth
carried out in body bags
in Uvalde, Texas
from a classroom
riddled with bullets
and populated by
an enormous elephant
nobody wants to address.

These poems are
the knees not bent to pray
-nor to propose marriage
but bent to protest police brutality

Or perhaps these poems are
the knee on the neck
of a black man
for more than nine minutes
-by a policeman sworn to protect and serve.

These poems are the somber eyes
of migrant kids in cages
of people fleeing a high school graduation
of mourners at a Maryland cemetery
during the burial of a murdered
10-year-old gun-violence victim
witnessing yet another mass shooting

Or, perhaps these poems are the somber eyes
staring at streets strewn with dead bodies
-the carnage from 14 mass shootings
this past bloody Memorial Day weekend
leaving eight dead and fifty-nine wounded.

These poems are
heavy and loaded
like the caskets we carry
like the bodies we bury.

JohnnieRenee Nia Nelson
Poet-Teacher, San Diego County

Angels in Unexpected Places

It's hard to know how angels
have saved me from my own dark thoughts
when doubts have piled high like landfills full of trash.
But I want to believe they pulled me out of my fear
when waiting for mammogram results
or hearing the startling siren of a cop car
pulling me over for a random traffic violation.
I want to believe they are there
when I hear the mourning dove coo eerily
in early morning like she is sad,
but then takes flight into the rare blue
sky of winter.

I want Gabriel to bring me a message
wrapped in origami. When I unfold it,
it spells POSSIBILITY and FRIENDLY UNIVERSE
that lifts my spine up like a back brace
so I walk with ease on this earthy plane.
I want to know how the spider has the tenacity
to keep weaving its web after I repeatedly
brush it out the kitchen corner
or the miracle of throwing a line
of its thread 6 feet out connecting two trees.
Angels shapeshift into creatures of nature.

Although I cannot touch their robes
or hear the pluck of their harps,
they appear in unlikely places

revealing that sliver of hope on the horizon,
and for a moment I feel held like a child
embraced by the softest feathery wings.

Terri Glass
Poet-Teacher, Del Norte and Marin County

Beholder

On this morning's trek a flute-winged jay
tipped and dove above the trail.
Last night's rain had licked the pavement clean,
flushed my atoms into rock and plank and loam.

I remembered the unit I taught on vision,
how afraid I was to
reveal the dark secret to ten-year-olds
as if outing the Easter Bunny.

How a bird's color enters the pupil a dull gray
before the image is absorbed like salt in water
in the organs of our eyes,
reflecting a breathless red or blue.

I longed to skirt this truth
but the sacrament of organs on my doorstep—
gift of the tabby—
whispered buck up; it's only science.

I flash on the Rufus Hummingbird,
Cardinal, Golden Oriole, and Scrub Jay,
and picture Gaia pulling wavelengths from a hat.
The House Wren always draws the shortest straw.

Sandra Anfang
Poet-Teacher, Sonoma County

Musical Personification

I am Music, the beat of life,
The rhythm of the heart, the soul's sweet strife.
I'm the melody that soothes your mind,
The lyrics that make your heart unwind.
I am the symphony of sound,
The harmony that's all around,
The notes that rise and fall in tune,
The chords that play beneath the moon.
I'm the voice that speaks to you,
The sound that makes your dreams come true,
The laughter that you can't ignore,
The tears that fall and then restore.
I am the rhythm that sets you free,
The bass that makes you want to be,
The music that you can't resist,
The song that always will persist.
So listen close and hear my call,
Let your heart and soul enthrall,
And when you hear me, you will see,
That I am Music, and I am thee.
I am the vibrant symphony of life,
The crescendo in a world of noise,
A guitar string that resonates with emotion,
The melody that dances in your heart.
I am the tender whispers of a piano,
The thunderous roar of drums,
A saxophone that sings the blues,

The harmony of voices blending together.
I am the passion of a rock concert,
The soulful rhythm of a jazz club,
The exhilarating beat of electronic dance,
And the nostalgic warmth of an old vinyl record.
I am the music that breathes life,
Into every moment,
And reminds us all,
That we are connected through sound.

Andrea Lee
Poet-Teacher, Los Angeles County

Unveiled Secret

I am wind down the throat of the flute. The wind that parts my
hair down the side from the current of Saul's breath, as he sings
Viento into life. The sweetness of our heartbeats collecting under
their song – umbrella of harmony – that fire of life – vida cleansed
– un limpia sacredo –
a fire that licks out the flauta
like a tongue tasting truth.
Serpiente, como tu sangre, traveling veins since the beaming of
your time – eyes awake, alert – witness to the water rising over
your eyes; the soft tide that sweeps your ankles.
The pads of your feet wear down with every stomp –
splash out to bless the frogs,
splash out to greet the timid beetles, grasshoppers, and bees;
splash out to bless the seed as it settles into its pick of earth.
Mira la lengua! Curled tight splashing
palabra that only you know – the wisdom shak- en into your
heart; that keeps these sounds etched into your ears.
Your quiet timing, in-step with your path, unfolding for you to
hold – whispers your name. Tell the story to the wind,
for your journey to live on.

Jessica M. Wilson
Poet-Teacher, Los Angeles County

Blue

is the color least found in nature, according to science,
but I suspect a bias in the spectrum. Lenses can now
show the range of colors seen by birds, spiders, reptiles—
Life does not see the world equally. Question the lens.
Remember your filters & what they leave behind. Have
you tried a new dilation today? Have you held a new
prism to your possibly yellow eye? When I see you
through love, I can see stars in your skin, an intricate
ethereal design, infinite stitches without a seam, ripple
streaks instead of footprints, reaching for the sea.

I see all the flowers you pass blooming
& all the petals are blue.

Brennan DeFrisco
Poet-Teacher, Alameda & Sonoma County

My Tío

Sharpening a blue color pencil with a sharp knife
for my baby daughter, I remembered mi Tío Memo
showing me how to do it.
No machine would get close to his perfection;
him holding the wooden handle, to give that pencil
the edge to paint the heavens,
an edge worthy of the hands of the painting gods.
Yellow, wooden bits, flying into the trash can,
led powder fogging up the scene of transformation.
His universe composed of charcoal shades and acrylics.
Portraits of Cardinals and Popes,
Virgin Marys and crosses,
in disbelief of such a revelation;
the secret of mastery.
I stopped wondering why,
and I widen my pupils to write it,
in the diary of my mind.

Juan Cárdenas
Poet-Teacher, Los Angeles County

My Tilde

My tilde is the debate of the decade
Calls for a crowd to surround me when I answer
Whether it belongs in my name or not
Because if this isn't the concern in question
They will instead ask whether I belong at all
Because it can only be unnatural to have
A name that cannot be pronounced one way
Dare I say the right way
Which is to say
The white way
But anyway
I tell them my tilde is like the grandmother
I'm not sure how I am related to
But all the same we share history
She tells me about the country we came from
And all the ways she saved up enough money
To cross over into this place that wonders to this day
Whether she is a construct that can be changed
Or a language that can be forgotten
I ask her why she was not there when I was born
And she replies that the doctors didn't want her
To hold a child who did not resemble her
Still, I heard her calling to me each night
Claiming me as hers and asking to be mine
"Todos los demás me han olvidado
Eres la única que puede llevar mi legado"
I do not know when she died

Or if she ever did at all
Only that she disappeared for generations
Chose me as the one to carry her legacy
And had me promise that no matter who asks
I will tell them that she always belongs
I'd rather be expelled for the spelling of my name
Than allow it to ever again be erased

Angelina Leaños
Poet-Teacher, Ventura County
Youth Poet Laureate Emeritus

Peace Be Kind

Think peace and be kind
a clarion call for this time
of unprecedented endurance
The world both smaller
and bigger as we
lift the goggles
to repel the frequency skirmishes
and sundry manipulations
designed to thwart our coming together

yet these rays of ourselves
are meant to shine
illuminate the sun path
making us impossible to stop
no matter how fierce the storm
our epicenter knows how to survive
when we moor our minds to sky
and fasten our feet to earth
knowing we all want
the same thing
even if we call it something different

peace as the sunset affirms
another day of belonging
love as it rises before our eyes
in the light of morning
stability as the moon dances
above the tallest redwood

We are a wave vaster than
any division
any particle
a mural of rainbow proportions
stretching as far as our imagination
and our tenderness
belies our strength

we are a crystal megaphone
roiling and ringing
within the cauldron
of this human vulnerability

and we must embrace tolerance
the science of heart math
if we wish to survive
into the intimacy of telling our visions
spelling out
our compassion
grasping that there is
no sweetness
when hearts have hate
no melody
when mouths spill anger
no sustenance
when intolerance fogs our head
no rest when we go to sleep
unsettled

so here we are

rising up within ourselves
gathering like a solar system
extending its concentric revolutions
into a cosmos of understanding

It has been a long three years
since we gathered like this
our celebrations shifting
we have all lost something
it is our common denominator
our initiation to empathy
we have what it takes
we know it
and here we are
still alive
opening ourselves to the world
we nearly let go
hugging each other
inviting friends back to our tables
this tender community
realizing the only way out
is through
looking into the horror
and recognizing its beauty
the age of Aquarius
has dawned
now it is up
to us
to live it

Blake More

Poet-Teacher, Mendocino County

Acknowledgements

California Poets in the Schools extends our overwhelming gratitude to all the agencies, arts foundations, and contributors that made this publication possible, including the California Arts Council.

Special thanks to all the administrators, teachers, librarians, and literacy coaches who welcome our Poet-Teachers into their schools and classrooms. Thank you for providing and sharing the space for our poetry workshops.

Thank you to all the CalPoets coordinators and Poet-Teachers whose knowledge, facilitation and artistic guidance catalyzed the creation of this anthology and all the poems written beyond these pages. Thank you for all you do.

A cacophony of applause to all our student poet contributors for sharing your words, your selves, and your literary brilliance with all of us through this collection. Thank you for you.

& thank you, reader, for spending time with these poems.

California Poets in the Schools' vision is to enable youth in every California county to discover, cultivate and amplify their own creative voices through reading, analyzing, writing, performing and publishing poetry. When students learn to express their creativity, imagination, and intellectual curiosity through poetry, it becomes a catalyst for learning core academic subjects, accelerating emotional development and supporting personal growth. Our Poet-Teachers help students become adults who will bring compassion, understanding and appreciation for diverse perspectives to dialogue about issues which their communities face.

California Poets in the Schools (CalPoets) develops and empowers a multicultural network of independent Poet- Teachers, who bring the many benefits of poetry to youth throughout the state. As a membership network we offer opportunities for professional development, peer learning and fundraising assistance for Poet-Teachers in California. We also cultivate relationships with school districts, foundations and arts organizations which can fund and support our members' professional practices.

Since 1964, CalPoets has grown to become one of the oldest and largest writers-in-the-schools programs in the nation. Our reach includes over 10,000 students served annually by 60 Poet-Teachers from throughout California. Poet-Teachers live and serve students K-12 in over 20 California counties, stretching from Humboldt and Siskiyou to Los Angeles and San Diego, in districts both urban and rural. Each year, CalPoets' Poet-Teachers reach hundreds of classrooms, teaching in public and private schools, juvenile halls, after-school programs, hospitals and other community settings.

CalPoets champions and amplifies the voices of California youth by providing platforms for critical literacy, youth development & leadership through school-based poetry writing, publication and performance opportunities.

To Contact CalPoets for a residency:

Phone – 1-415-221-4201
Email – *info@cpits.org*
Website – *www.californiapoets.org*

Printed in the USA
CPSIA information can be obtained
at www.ICGtesting.com
CBHW050747111123
1767CB00003B/3